More than Cool Reason

More than Cool Reason
A Field Guide to Poetic Metaphor

George Lakoff and Mark Turner

The University of Chicago Press   Chicago and London

The University of Chicago Press, Chicago 60637
The University of Chicago Press, Ltd., London
© 1989 by The University of Chicago
All rights reserved. Published 1989
Printed in the United States of America

15 14 13 12 11 10 09 08 07 06   9 10 11 12 13

Library of Congress Cataloging-in-Publication Data

Lakoff, George.
  More than cool reason : a field guide to poetic metaphor / George
Lakoff and Mark Turner.
  p. cm.
  Bibliography: p.
  Includes index.
  ISBN 0-226-46812-7 (pbk.)
  1. Metaphor. 2. Poetics. 3. Languages—Philosophy. I. Turner,
Mark, 1954–   . II. Title.
PN228.M4L27   1989
808.1—dc19   88-29306
                                                            CIP

To Claudia and Andy and to Megan

Contents

Acknowledgments

Our highest thanks to Claudia Brugman for help of every sort in writing this book. Our thanks for ideas and criticism to Michele Emanatian, Gary Holland, Mark Johnson, Chana Kronfeld, Bettina Nicely, and Eve Sweetser, and to Jane Espenson, who also helped with editing and indexing. Special thanks go to Jerome Rothenberg for both ideas and examples. We thank Greg Meagher and Kiki Nikiforidou for examples. Many of the ideas in this book were developed during class discussions with the students of a seminar in metaphor we taught jointly at Berkeley in spring, 1987. Mark Turner taught a near-final draft of the book to students at the University of Chicago in autumn, 1987, as did George Lakoff to students at the University of California at Berkeley. We thank them for their help in improving the text.

Without the tradition of scholarship of a group of metaphor researchers, this book would not have been possible. We would like to thank William Nagy and Michael Reddy for their pioneering and too-little-known work, Mark Johnson, who co-authored *Metaphors We Live By* with George Lakoff, and who has since done further major research on metaphor, and Claudia Brugman, Naomi Quinn, and Eve Sweetser for subsequent work that has provided us with many ideas.

Mark Turner would like to thank the NEH for a fellowship for independent research, which he held during the year this book was written. We would both like to thank the Sloan Foundation and the Institute for Cognitive Studies for providing research equipment and facilities and a rich intellectual environment.

Permission to reprint the following is gratefully acknowledged: Dylan Thomas's "Do not go gentle into that good night" (*The Poems of Dylan Thomas;* copyright 1952 by Dylan Thomas; by permission of New Directions Publishing Corp. and Dent & Sons, Ltd.); William Carlos Williams's "To a Solitary Disciple" (*Collected Poems, Volume 1: 1909–1939;* copyright 1938 by New Directions Publishing Corp.; reprinted by permission of Carcanet Press, Ltd.); and W. S. Merwin's *Asian Figures* (reprinted with permission of Atheneum Publishers, an imprint of Macmillan Publishing Co.; copyright © 1971, 1972, 1973, by W. S. Merwin; reprinted by permission of Georges Borchardt, Inc., for the author; copyright © 1973 by W. S. Merwin).

Preface

It is commonly thought that poetic language is beyond ordinary language—that it is something essentially different, special, higher, with extraordinary tools and techniques like metaphor and metonymy, instruments beyond the reach of someone who just talks. But great poets, as master craftsmen, use basically the same tools we use; what makes them different is their talent for using these tools, and their skill in using them, which they acquire from sustained attention, study, and practice.

Metaphor is a tool so ordinary that we use it unconsciously and automatically, with so little effort that we hardly notice it. It is omnipresent: metaphor suffuses our thoughts, no matter what we are thinking about. It is accessible to everyone: as children, we automatically, as a matter of course, acquire a mastery of everyday metaphor. It is conventional: metaphor is an integral part of our ordinary everyday thought and language. And it is irreplaceable: metaphor allows us to understand our selves and our world in ways that no other modes of thought can.

Far from being merely a matter of words, metaphor is a matter of thought—all kinds of thought: thought about emotion, about society, about human character, about language, and about the nature of life and death. It is indispensable not only to our imagination but also to our reason.

Great poets can speak to us because they use the modes of thought we all possess. Using the capacities we all share, poets can illuminate our experience, explore the consequences of our beliefs, challenge the ways we think, and criticize our ideologies. To understand the nature and value of poetic creativity requires us to understand the ordinary ways we think.

Because metaphor is a primary tool for understanding our world and our selves, entering into an engagement with powerful poetic metaphors is grappling in an important way with what it means to have a human life.

We have written this book to analyze the role of metaphor in poetry. In it, we take up general questions of the theory of metaphor, and, more widely, questions of rhetoric, meaning, and reasoning. The book should therefore prove valuable to students and researchers in literature, linguistics, philosophy, psychology, anthropology, and cognitive science.

We have tried to write the book in a style accessible to undergraduates who are learning to read poetry in depth. We hope it will help them to understand how poetic metaphor works.

ONE

Life, Death, and Time

"Because I could not stop for Death"

Because I could not stop for Death—
He kindly stopped for me—
The Carriage held but just Ourselves—
And Immortality.

Metaphors are so commonplace we often fail to notice them. Take the way we ordinarily talk about death. The euphemism "He passed away" is not an arbitrary one. When someone dies, we don't say "He drank a glass of milk" or "He had an idea" or "He upholstered his couch." Instead we say things like "He's gone," "He's left us," "He's no longer with us," "He's passed on," "He's been taken from us," "He's gone to the great beyond," and "He's among the dear departed." All of these are mundane, and they are metaphoric. They are all instances of a general metaphorical way we have of conceiving of birth, life, and death in which BIRTH IS ARRIVAL, LIFE IS BEING PRESENT HERE, and DEATH IS DEPARTURE. Thus, we speak of a baby being "on the way" and "a little bundle from heaven," and we send out announcements of its "arrival." When Shakespeare's King Lear says

Thou must be patient, we came crying hither:
Thou know'st the first time that we smell the air
We waul and cry . . . (*King Lear*, 4.4)

he is using an extension of the very ordinary metaphorical conception of birth as arrival ("came hither") that we use when we speak of a baby being on the way. Mark Twain said he "came in" with Halley's comet and would "go out"

1

with it—and we all understand that he was talking about birth and death. To speak of someone, after a serious operation, as being "still with us" is to say he is alive, with the "still" suggesting the possibility of imminent departure. Someone who is "at Death's door" can be spoken of as "slipping away." If a patient's heart stops beating and a doctor gets it started again, the doctor can describe this as "bringing him back." And if a doctor, after an operation, emerges from the operating room and says "We lost him," then we know the patient died, because something that is lost is absent.

All this may seem obvious, but there is an important theoretical issue at stake in these examples: metaphor resides in thought, not just in words. There is a metaphorical conception of death as departure that can be expressed in many different ways, such as "passing away," "being gone," and "departing." Though we would not normally speak of a coachman coming to take away someone who is dying, we nonetheless normally conceive of death as a departure and speak of it that way. And when Emily Dickinson speaks of Death as a coachman, she is using an extension of the same general and ordinary metaphorical conception of death as departure that we use when we speak of someone passing away.

We use the death-as-departure metaphor in making sense of Dickinson's poem. We can see this by noticing that nowhere in the first four lines is anything said about departure with no return. And yet we know when she says, "The Carriage held but just Ourselves" that the passengers are not simply sitting in the carriage or going for a visit or a spin around the block. We know because we understand death as a departure with no return. Because we conceive of death in this way, Dickinson does not need to state all of the details: we know them by virtue of knowing the basic conceptual metaphor.

Life and death are such all-encompassing matters that there can be no single conceptual metaphor that will enable us to comprehend them. There is a multiplicity of metaphors for life and death, and a number of the most common ones show up in the Dickinson poem. To begin to sort them out, let us return to the line "Because I could not stop for Death—." We understand here that what the speaker cannot stop are her purposeful activities. A purposeful life has goals, and one searches for means toward those goals. We conceive metaphorically of purposes as destinations and of the means to those destinations as paths. We speak of "going ahead with our plans," "getting sidetracked," "doing things in a roundabout way," and "working our way around obstacles." Thus there is a common metaphor PURPOSES ARE DESTINATIONS, and such expressions are instances of it.

When we think of life as purposeful, we think of it as having destinations and paths toward those destinations, which makes life a journey. We can speak of children as "getting off to a good start" in life and of the aged as being "at the end of the trail." We describe people as "making their way in life." People worry about whether they "are getting anywhere" with their lives, and about "giving their lives some direction." People who "know where they're going in life" are generally admired. In discussing options, one may say "I don't know which path to take." When Robert Frost says,

> Two roads diverged in a wood, and I—
> I took the one less traveled by,
> And that has made all the difference,
> ("The Road Not Taken")

we typically read him as discussing options for how to live life, and as claiming that he chose to do things differently than most other people do.

This reading comes from our implicit knowledge of the structure of the LIFE IS A JOURNEY metaphor. Knowing the structure of this metaphor means knowing a number of correspondences between the two conceptual domains of life and journeys, such as these:

— The person leading a life is a traveler.
— His purposes are destinations.
— The means for achieving purposes are routes.
— Difficulties in life are impediments to travel.
— Counselors are guides.
— Progress is the distance traveled.

3

— Things you gauge your progress by are landmarks.
— Choices in life are crossroads.
— Material resources and talents are provisions.

We will speak of such a set of correspondences as a "mapping" between two conceptual domains. Thus we will speak, for example, of destinations being mapped onto purposes.

When we read "Because I could not stop for Death—" and understand that what the speaker could not stop are her purposeful activities, we can understand those purposes as destinations and her life as a journey to reach those destinations. The occurrence of the word "Death" in the line suggests the reading that what she declines to stop is her life's journey. The second line, "He kindly stopped for me," and the occurrence of "Carriage" in the third line make it clear that what is being talked about is a journey.

Life is a journey with a stopping point, and that stopping point is death's departure point. Consequently, death too can involve a journey with a destination. So we speak of going to the great beyond, a better place, our final resting place, the last roundup. In Greek mythology, when you die, the ferryman Charon carries you from the shore of the river Styx across to the underworld. In Christian mythology, you ascend to the pearly gates or descend to the gates of hell. Other religious traditions, such as ancient Egyptian, also conceive of death as a departure on a journey. So, when Tennyson discusses death he refers to it as "when I put out to sea." When John Keats, discussing death, says "then on the shore / Of this wide world I stand alone," we understand that the shore is death's departure point, and that land's end is life's end.

Dickinson's coachman is taking her on death's journey, as we can see in the full poem:

> Because I could not stop for Death—
> He kindly stopped for me—
> The Carriage held but just Ourselves—
> And Immortality.
>
> We slowly drove—He knew no haste
> And I had put away

My labor and my leisure too,
For his Civility—
We passed the School, where Children strove
At Recess—in the Ring—
We passed the Fields of Gazing Grain—
We passed the Setting Sun—

Or rather—He passed Us—
The Dews drew quivering and chill—
For only Gossamer, my Gown—
My Tippet—only Tulle—

We paused before a House that seemed
A Swelling of the Ground—
The Roof was scarcely visible—
The Cornice—in the Ground—

Since then—'tis Centuries—and yet
Feels shorter than the Day
I first surmised the Horses' Heads
Were toward Eternity.

In this poem, Death is taking the speaker on a journey, and the first part of the journey reviews the stages of life that one traverses during life's journey. We interpret the children at school as referring to the stage of childhood, the field of ripe crops as referring to full maturity, the setting sun as referring to old age, the dews and chill and the near darkness suggested by the phrase "scarcely visible" as referring to the onset of death, and the swelling of the ground as referring to the final home of the body—the grave, the end of life's journey.

How do we understand so easily and naturally that the sequence of things the speaker mentions refers to the sequence of life-stages, to childhood, maturity, old age, death? The answer, in part, is that we know unconsciously and automatically many basic metaphors for understanding life, and Dickinson relies on our knowledge of these metaphors to lead us to connect the sequence she gives to the sequence of life-stages. As we shall see, we use the basic metaphor PEOPLE ARE PLANTS to understand that the "Fields of Gazing Grain" suggests maturity. We use the basic metaphor A LIFETIME IS A DAY to understand both that the setting sun refers to old age and that the dew and chill and near darkness refer to the onset of death. In understanding the swelling of the ground as referring to the final "home" of the body, we use both what we will call an "image-metaphor" and the basic metaphor DEATH IS GOING TO A FINAL DESTINATION. Let us see how each of these metaphors works in detail.

PEOPLE ARE PLANTS

In this metaphor, people are viewed as plants with respect to the life cycle—more precisely, they are viewed as that part of the plant that burgeons and then withers or declines, such as leaves, flowers, and fruit, though sometimes the whole plant is viewed as burgeoning and then declining, as with grass or wheat. As Psalm 103 says, "As for man, his days are as grass: as a flower of the field, so he flourisheth." Death comes with the harvest and the falling of the leaves. The stages of the plants and parts of plants in their yearly cycle correspond to the stages of life. When we speak of someone as "a young sprout," we mean that he is in the early stages of life. Someone "in full bloom" is mature. Someone "withering away" is approaching death. Wheat that has put forth its grain is mature. Thus, in the Dickinson poem, we can apply the PEOPLE ARE PLANTS metaphor to read the "Fields of Gazing Grain" as referring to a stage of life—maturity.

A LIFETIME IS A DAY

In this metaphor, birth is dawn, maturity is noon, old age is twilight, the moment of death is sunset, and the state of death is night. Via this metaphor, Dickinson's line about the "setting sun" can be understood as referring to old age. In our conventional schema for a day, as the sun sets, the dew and chill set in. Metaphorically, death's coldness is night's coldness, since death is night. Against the coldness of death coming on, the speaker has only a gossamer gown and a very thin shawl (a tippet made of tulle, a very fine cloth).

DEATH IS GOING TO A FINAL DESTINATION

We conceive of death as something to which we are all subject. Death is inevitable and final. Particular deaths may vary in certain details; one may "go out" in a variety of fashions. Correspondingly, the DEATH IS DEPARTURE metaphor does not fix the details of how one departs: for example, one may depart in a carriage, a boat, or a chariot. But since one inevitably dies, so the metaphorical departure is inevitable, as is the final state to which it leads.

The death-as-departure metaphor is often extended in religious traditions, where the departure is seen as the beginning of a journey to a final destination. This makes use of the basic metaphor that STATES ARE LOCATIONS that one can be in, enter, or leave. Being dead is a final state, and therefore, metaphorically, a final location. A change of state is metaphorically a change of location. Via DEATH IS DEPARTURE, this final location is the final destination toward which one departs. The specific details of this final location vary: it can be, for example, God the Father's house, punishment in hell, an assigned spot in the underworld, final rest, or the place of one's origin, which can be one's home.

If one conceives of the earth as where the body comes from and returns to and belongs, then one can conceive of the grave as the home, not just the house, of the body. Then going to the grave can be going home: "Dust thou art, and unto dust shalt thou return" (Genesis 3:19). Home is where you start from and return to, and it is where you belong. In the Judeo-Christian conception, our soul comes from God the Father, and it returns to our Father's house, as in John 14:2: "in my Father's house are many mansions . . . I go to prepare a place for you."

We apply the DEATH IS GOING TO A FINAL DESTINATION metaphor to understand the Dickinson poem as presenting death in terms of a departure from this life and a journey toward a final destination, namely, the grave. The scarcely visible "House" she mentions is her grave, the final residence of the body, in which the body will dwell. The carriage is the hearse, moving slowly, with "no haste." The

7

gossamer gown is her death shroud. There is an image-metaphor at work in these lines, which helps to activate the DEATH IS GOING TO A FINAL DESTINATION metaphor. Our conventional image of a grave is superimposed on our conventional image of a house: the roof of the house is the bulge of earth, and the cornice of the roof is the gravestone, with the interior of the house being earth. Such a superimposition of images constitutes a metaphor in itself, since it is a mapping from one conventional image onto another conventional image. Such an image-metaphor can then help activate other conceptual metaphors. Because our conventional image of a grave is associated with death and our conventional image of a house is associated with our going toward our own houses as final destinations, the superimposition of the images activates a connection between death and going home, and hence it activates the metaphor DEATH IS GOING TO A FINAL DESTINATION.

We have thus seen five basic metaphors for death that are used naturally, automatically, and largely unconsciously in understanding the Dickinson poem. They are DEATH IS THE END OF LIFE'S JOURNEY, DEATH IS DEPARTURE (an inference from LIFE IS BEING PRESENT HERE), DEATH IS NIGHT (from A LIFETIME IS A DAY), HUMAN DEATH IS THE DEATH OF A PLANT, such as the harvesting of grain, the falling of leaves from the tree, and so on (from PEOPLE ARE PLANTS), and DEATH IS GOING TO A FINAL DESTINATION (an instance of CHANGE OF STATE IS CHANGE OF LOCATION).

Dickinson extended and composed these metaphors in novel ways. But, though she created the poem, she did not create the basic metaphors on which the poem is based. They were already there for her, widespread throughout Western culture, in the everyday thought of the least literate of people as well as in the greatest poetry in her traditions.

Some Conceptions of Life and Death

It is important to distinguish the way we conceive metaphorically of such things as life and death from the way a particular poet may express such thoughts in language. We began this book with "Because I could not stop for Death" not to focus particularly on that poem as opposed to a multitude of others but to illustrate some basic metaphors that belong to our culture. We all use them.

General conceptual metaphors are thus not the unique creation of individual poets but are rather part of the way members of a culture have of conceptualizing their experience. Poets, as members of their cultures, naturally make use of these basic conceptual metaphors to communicate with other members, their audience. Therefore, we would expect the basic metaphors used by Dickinson to show up in the works of many other poets. Let us consider how other poets use each of these basic metaphors.

LIFE IS A JOURNEY

Dante begins his *Divine Comedy*:

> In the middle of life's road,
> I found myself in a dark wood.

We understand, by virtue of the LIFE IS A JOURNEY metaphor, that somewhere during maturity, the speaker found himself in a condition of being "lost," that is, without clear purpose in life or a clear path to his purpose.

Shakespeare too sees life as a journey that ends in death:

> And all our yesterdays have lighted fools
> The way to dusty death.
> (*Macbeth* 5.5)

When Jesus says, in Matthew 7:13–14,

> Enter ye in at the strait gate: for wide is the gate, and broad is the way, that leadeth to destruction, and many there be which go in thereat: because strait is the gate, and narrow is the way, which leadeth unto life, and few there be that find it,

we understand that he is referring to alternative paths through life which lead to different destinations in the hereafter.

The allegory of Bunyan's *Pilgrim's Progress* is similarly based on the life-as-a-journey metaphor, as summed up in the line:

As I walked through the wilderness of this world.

And perhaps the most famous use of the life-as-a-journey metaphor occurs in the twenty-third psalm, whose first line is "The Lord is my shepherd":

> He leadeth me in the paths of righteousness for his name's sake. Yea, though I walk through the valley of the shadow of death, I will fear no evil: for thou art with me; thy rod and thy staff they comfort me . . . Surely goodness and mercy shall follow me all the days of my life: and I will dwell in the house of the Lord forever.

The life-as-a-journey metaphor is so taken for granted in the Judeo-Christian tradition that we instantly understand that God is a guide, that there are alternative paths of good and evil through life, and that death hangs over us throughout.

One of our major ways of conceiving of ethical behavior is an elaboration of the life-as-a-journey metaphor: there are paths of righteousness and evil ways. Laws are viewed as prescribing paths through life to be followed. As Proverbs 16:25 says:

> There is a way that seemeth right unto a man, but the end thereof are the ways of death.

Death is Departure

Dickinson's coachman is paralleled by T. S. Eliot's footman:

> I have seen the moment of my greatness flicker,
> And I have seen the eternal Footman hold my coat,
>   and snicker,
> And in short, I was afraid.
> ("The Love Song of J. Alfred Prufrock")

Though neither death nor departure is explicitly mentioned in Eliot's lines, both are evoked by the "eternal Footman." We understand that the person to be carried in the carriage corresponds metaphorically to the person leading a life. The departure of the carriage corresponds to dying. And an agent who helps you depart, the footman, is a personification of death.

If death is a departure, there can be departure points, such as doors, in:

> Death hath a thousand doors to let out life.
> (Philip Massinger, *A Very Woman*)

And there can be means of departure, such as ships or rafts, as in these examples:

> Swift has sailed into his rest
> (W. B. Yeats, "Swift's Epitaph")

> We are all driven to the same place—
> sooner or later, each one's lot is tossed
> from the urn—the lot which will come out
> and will put us into the eternal exile of the raft.
> (Horace, bk. 2, Carmen 2.25–28.)

Death is actually understood as a particular kind of departure, namely, a departure which is one way, with no return, as we see in:

> "You know how little while we have to stay,
> And, once departed, may return no more."
> (Edward Fitzgerald, *The Rubáiyát of Omar Khayyám*)

There may be a direction to the departure, such as an ascent or a descent:

> Ah, make the most of what ye yet may spend,
> Before we too into the Dust descend;
> Dust into Dust, and under Dust, to lie,
> Sans wine, sans Song, sans Singer, and—sans End.
> (Fitzgerald, *The Rubáiyát*)

And the departure can be a mass ritualistic procession, as in

> The pungent oranges and bright, green wings
> Seem things in some procession of the dead,
> Winding across wide water, without sound.
> (Wallace Stevens, "Sunday Morning")

A LIFETIME IS A DAY

Dylan Thomas uses the lifetime-as-a-day metaphor as the basis of his classic "Do Not Go Gentle into That Good Night":

> Do not go gentle into that good night,
> Old age should burn and rave at close of day;
> Rage, rage against the dying of the light.

Via the metaphor A LIFETIME IS A DAY, we understand that the good night refers to death, and that the close of day and the dying of the light refer to the brief span just before death.

Tennyson presents death as occurring at sunset:

> Sunset and evening star,
> And one clear call for me!
> ("Crossing the Bar")

We see stages of life corresponding to stages of the day in:

> Alice grown lazy, mammoth but not fat,
> Declines upon her lost and twilight age.
> (Allen Tate, "The Last Days of Alice")

Morning corresponds to youth, and the movement of the sun to the progress of life:

> Now therefore, while the youthful hue
> Sits on thy skin like morning dew . . .
> . . . .
> Now let us sport us while we may, . . .
> . . . .
> Thus, though we cannot make our sun
> Stand still, yet we will make him run.
> (Andrew Marvell, "To His Coy Mistress")

As Catullus says,

> Suns can set and return again,
> but when our brief light goes out,
> there's one perpetual night to be slept through
> (Catullus 5.4–7).

PEOPLE ARE PLANTS

A standard way of understanding and talking about the life cycle is in terms of a metaphor according to which people are plants or parts of plants and a human life corresponds to a plant's life cycle.

In book six of the *Iliad*, Diomedes, confronting Glaukos

on the battlefield, asks Glaukos to identify himself. Glaukos at first indicates that his identity doesn't matter, by saying:

> Why ask my birth, Diomedes? Very like leaves
> upon this earth are the generations of men—
> old leaves, cast on the ground by wind, young leaves
> the greening forest bears when spring comes in.
> So mortals pass; one generation flowers
> even as another dies away.
> (Trans. Robert Fitzgerald)

What Glaukos is saying is that one soldier is like any other, just as one leaf is indistinguishable from another, and generations of leaves come and go.

The stages of the plants and parts of plants in their yearly cycle correspond to the stages of life—bud to youth, full leaf to maturity, and withered leaf to old age:

> I have lived long enough. My way of life
> Is fallen into the sere, the yellow leaf.
> And that which should accompany old age,
> As honour, love, obedience, troops of friends,
> I must not look to have.
> (*Macbeth* 5.3)

Though leaves grow naturally, some plants, such as wheat, are cultivated, and must be sown and harvested. Thus, being harvested corresponds in the people-as-plants metaphor to the moment of death:

> . . . what inexorable cause
> Makes Time so vicious in his reaping.
> (Edward Arlington Robinson, "For a Dead Lady")

Offspring are the seed of parents, and the stages of life correspond to the seasonal stages of grain:

> Thou shalt know also that thy seed shall be great,
> and thy offspring as the grass of the earth.
> Thou shalt come to thy grave in a full age,
> like as a shock of corn cometh in in his season.
> (Job 5:25–26)

To be cut down is to die:

Man that is born of woman . . . cometh forth like a
flower,
and is cut down. (Job 14:1–2)

DEATH IS GOING TO A FINAL DESTINATION

As we mentioned above, there are many possible final locations, some of which are conceived of as places from which
one began. One such place of beginning and final return is
home, as in these lines:

> Fear no more the heat o' th' sun
> Nor the furious winter's rages;
> Thou thy worldly task hast done,
> Home art gone, and ta'en thy wages.
> Golden lads and girls all must,
> As chimney-sweepers, come to dust.
> (Shakespeare, *Cymbeline* 4.2)

We come, almost literally, from our mother's lap, and we
also come from earth. Dying, then, can be returning to
earth, and metaphorically to one's mother's lap:

> How gladly would I meet
> Mortality, my sentence, and be earth
> Insensible! how glad would lay me down
> As in my mother's lap!
> (John Milton, *Paradise Lost* bk. 10).

In Psalm 23, although no mention is made of departure,
we can easily understand, by virtue of the metaphor of
death as a departure for a final location, that one leaves the
earthly "valley of the shadow of death" and goes to live in
the house of the Lord:

> Surely goodness and mercy shall follow me all the
>   days of my life: and I will dwell in the house of the
>   Lord for ever.

When, in a different poem, Dickinson writes

> Afraid? Of whom am I afraid?
> Not Death, for who is He?
> The porter of my father's lodge
> As much abasheth me . . .

we understand that the father's lodge, which is home, is the soul's final resting place after death, and that the porter who ushers you into that home is death personified.

We hope that this section has made it clear that there exist basic conceptual metaphors for understanding life and death that are part of our culture and that we routinely use to make sense of the poetry of our culture. We might have used any of these poems as an introduction to these basic metaphors. We chose the Dickinson poem not to point out what is unusual about it but rather to introduce the range of common, unconscious, automatic basic metaphors which are part of our cultural knowledge and which allow us to communicate with each other, whether in ordinary conversation or in poetry.

Personifications of Death

We have seen so far that a very large number of metaphorical expressions for life and death throughout Western poetry are instances of a very small number of basic conceptual metaphors through which we comprehend life and death. In the same way, the many metaphorical *personifications* of death derive from the same small number of basic conceptual metaphors. Thus the porter can personify death in the above example by virtue of the basic metaphor DEATH IS GOING TO A FINAL DESTINATION. Dickinson identified the final location as her father's lodge, and the role of the porter is to help the traveler enter the location. Similarly, Eliot's eternal Footman and the coachman in Dickinson's "Because I could not stop for Death" also play the established roles of assisting the traveler to his final destination. These three functionaries thus all play corresponding roles in the journey. Where they differ is in the nature either of the journey itself or the character of the destination. Our escort may be the angel of death or the man who knocks at the door or anyone who comes to summon us to make that final journey. Thus, we understand the gentleman in the dustcoat in the following poem as one who summons the young lady in the poem to her death:

—I am a gentleman in a dustcoat trying
To make you hear. Your ears are soft and small
And listen to an old man not at all,
They want the young men's whispering and sighing.
But see the roses on your trellis dying
And hear the spectral singing of the moon;
For I must have my lovely lady soon,
I am a gentleman in a dustcoat trying.
(John Crowe Ransom, "Piazza Piece")

This interpretation is reinforced as we also bring to bear the metaphor PEOPLE ARE PLANTS in understanding the significance of the roses on the trellis dying. And we can use LIFE IS A DAY to take the moon as indicating night, and hence death.

It is typical of such personifications that, since they identify some factotum whose job is to assist the traveler, that actor is civil and gentlemanly. But there is a second class of personifications of death. The role of these personifications is not to escort or summon one to death but rather to effect the death. They too each derive from some basic conceptual metaphor. For example, the grim reaper is himself responsible for the death he brings about. The personification of death as grim reaper exists by virtue of the PEOPLE ARE PLANTS metaphor, in which people are plants which are harvested by the reaper.

Death personified can be an enemy one fights against. Dunbar presents death as a fully armed knight who cuts down all other warriors in the battle:

He [Death] takis the knichtis in to field
Enarmit under helm and scheild:
Victor he is at all mellie.

Here we have an instance of a basic metaphor for death that we have not yet discussed, DYING IS LOSING A CONTEST AGAINST AN ADVERSARY. It is part of a more general basic metaphor, STAYING ALIVE IS A CONTEST, which comes into play when the possibility of dying is contemplated. Just as there are kinds of contests, so there are special cases of this metaphor: a race, a wrestling match, armed combat, a struggle with a beast, a chess game. In any contest, one has an adversary, and this adversary can be personified as Death. Thus, Death can be seen as someone trying to catch you, a warrior battling you, a beast trying to devour you, or your opponent in a chess match. For example, Marvell, in "To His Coy Mistress," presents death as trying to catch us:

> But, at my back I always hear
> Time's wingèd chariot hurrying near.

1 Corinthians, 15 : 55 presents the contest as combat:

> O Death, where is thy sting? O grave, where
> is thy victory?

John Donne sees the contest as a struggle with a mighty and dreadful antagonist:

> Death be not proud, though some have called thee
> Mighty and dreadful, for thou art not so,
> For, those, whom thou think'st, thou dost overthrow,
> Die not, poor death, nor yet canst thou kill me . . .
> . . . .
> . . . death, thou shalt die.

Tennyson's adversary in the life-and-death struggle is a devouring beast:

> Into the jaws of death,
> Into the mouth of hell
> Rode the six hundred.
> ("Charge of the Light Brigade")

And the adversary can be an opponent in a footrace:

> Who can run the race with Death?
> (Samuel Johnson, Letter to Doctor Burney, 2 August
> 1784)

The structures of the basic metaphors provide the roles which can serve as the sources of personifications. This means that no separate personification metaphor is needed to account for these cases, and it also explains why the personifications of death are all either minions to assist one to a final destination, or agents who cause death, or both.

Other Metaphorical Conceptions of Death

Life and death are such all-encompassing concepts that we need many different conceptual tools for understanding and reasoning about them. There are a number of basic metaphors for comprehending life and death, and each of these metaphors focuses on different aspects, highlighting or downplaying them, and giving rise to different inferences, which often conflict. Before we consider some truly complex cases in great poetry, let us survey some of the most basic metaphors we have for making sense of life and death.

A LIFETIME IS A YEAR; DEATH IS WINTER

In this conception of the life cycle, springtime is youth, summer is maturity, autumn is old age, and winter is death. When Donne writes,

> No Spring, nor Summer beauty hath such grace,
> As I have seen in one Autumnal face
> ("Elegies," 9),

we understand that an autumnal face belongs to a certain season of life—old age. For Robert Browning, the coming of winter corresponds to the coming of death:

> Fear death?— to feel the fog in my throat,
> The mist in my face,
> When the snows begin, and the blasts denote
> I am nearing the place.
> ("Prospice")

This is a very natural metaphoric conception of life and death, since spring is the season in which new plant and animal life emerge while winter signals the dormancy or hibernation of plants and animals. Notice that this metaphor is coherent with one elaboration of the PEOPLE ARE PLANTS metaphor, where buds and new shoots correspond to birth or youth, and plant dormancy to death.

DEATH IS SLEEP

In this metaphor, the corpse corresponds to the body of a sleeper, and the appearance of the corpse—inactive and

18

inattentive—to the appearance of the sleeper. Optionally, the experiences of the soul after death correspond to our mental experiences during sleep, namely dreaming. And just as death is a particular sort of departure, a one-way departure with no return, so death is a particular sort of sleep, an eternal sleep from which we never waken. As Aristophanes says in *The Frogs*,

> For what is Death but an eternal sleep?

Hamlet, trying to understand death, conceives of it in terms of sleep:

> To die; to sleep;—
> To sleep? Perchance to dream! Ay, there's the rub;
> For in that sleep of death what dreams may come . . .

When sleep is conceived of as rest, death can be a final rest—one from which we will not wake, as in

> Lo! some we loved, the loveliest and the best
> That Time and Fate of all their Vintage prest,
> Have drunk their Cup a Round or two before,
> And one by one crept silently to Rest.
> (Fitzgerald, *The Rubáiyát*).

LIFE IS FLUID IN THE BODY; DEATH IS LOSS OF FLUID

In the Fitzgerald example above, we see not only that death is sleep but also that life is a fluid that can be crushed out of you ("all their Vintage prest"). In the LIFE IS A FLUID metaphor, the body corresponds to a container (a cup, a grape), and the life of the body corresponds to the fluid in the container. The intensity of life corresponds to the amount of fluid in the container. When the container breaks or is broken, the fluid escapes and the amount of fluid diminishes. Metaphorically, life diminishes. Death corresponds to the total absence of fluid in the container ("all their Vintage prest").

In the Fitzgerald example, fluid is crushed out. Alternatively, it can drain out, as in

> In headaches and in worry
> Vaguely life leaks away
> (W. H. Auden, "As I Walked Out One Evening"),

19

or flow out, as in these lines from the same poem:

> The glacier knocks in the cupboard,
> The desert sighs in the bed,
> And the crack in the tea-cup opens
> A lane to the land of the dead.

When "the crack in the tea-cup opens," life begins to flow out, which is metaphorically the onset of dying. In the LIFE IS BEING PRESENT HERE; DEATH IS DEPARTURE metaphor, starting out on the path "to the land of the dead" is also metaphorically the onset of dying. Because they play this same role, the overlap of images is natural: the stream of fluid out of the cup is a lane and therefore can be a lane to the land of the dead. Again, as in the case of the grave being a house, we have an image-metaphor, a mapping of one conventional image onto another. And again, the image-metaphor and conceptual metaphors are mutually reinforcing.

LIFE IS A PLAY

Everyday phrases like "It's curtains for him," "She's my leading lady," "She always wants to be in the spotlight," "The kid stole the show," "That's not in the script," "What's your part in this?," "You missed your cue," "He blew his lines," "He saved the show," "She brought the house down," and "Clean up your act!" all rely on our metaphoric understanding of significant parts of life (including the entire span of life) in terms of a play. This is an extraordinarily productive basic metaphor for life, perhaps because plays are often intended to *portray* significant events and parts of life, and the ways in which a play can be made to correspond to life are extensively developed and conventionalized in our culture. Our schema for a play is also very rich. It includes actors, make-up, costume, a stage, scenery, setting and lighting, audiences, scripts, parts, roles, cues, prompts, directors, casting, playwrights, applause, bowing, and so on. Very many of the components of the schema for play have a function in the LIFE IS A PLAY metaphor. We say "He always plays the fool," "That attitude is just a mask," "He turned in a great performance," "Take a bow!," "You deserve a standing ovation," "He plays an important role in the process," "He played only a bit part in my life," "He's waiting in the wings," "I'm improvising," "It's showtime!," "You're on!," and so on.

Plays prototypically have a formal structure (prologue, acts and scenes, intermission, epilogue, and so on). Thus we can refer to the beginning of something in life as "act one" or to a calm period as an "intermission." Elvis Presley refers in a popular song to the beginning of love by saying "Act one was when we met," and Frank Sinatra refers to contemplating imminent death by saying "And now I face the final curtain." Plays also prototypically have a narrative structure (introduction, complication, climax, and so on). Thus we can refer to the high point of a part of life as the "climax."

In the LIFE IS A PLAY metaphor, the person leading a life corresponds to an actor, the people with whom he interacts are fellow actors, his behavior is the way he is acting, and so on. If all of life is the span under consideration, then birth is the beginning of the play and the event of death is the falling of the curtain. If only a part of life is the span under consideration, then those components of our schema for play that take place before or after the actual performance can correspond to events before or after the part of life under consideration. For example, someone who is going to a job interview that he does not take seriously in order to practice his interviewing skills for a serious interview can say "this is just a rehearsal." Evaluators of ways we have behaved during a significant part of life can be understood in terms of critics who give rave reviews or who pan us. If we have received attention for our efforts in life, we can say "I've been in the spotlight."

This extremely productive metaphor for understanding life has been extended in Western culture in any number of ways. Epictetus, for example, asks us to think of the deity as the playwright who assigns us roles. Our business in life is to play admirably the role assigned to us.

Shakespeare has used this very common basic metaphor as the basis for famous passages like

All the world's a stage,
And all the men and women merely players.
They have their exits and their entrances;
And one man in his time plays many parts.
(*As You Like It* 2.7)

And Thomas Middleton has echoed him:

The world's a stage on which all parts are played.
("A Game of Chess")

We can understand the kind of life a person is suited to lead metaphorically in terms of the kind of roles an actor is suited to play, as in

No! I am not Prince Hamlet, nor was meant to be;
Am an attendant lord, one that will do
To swell a progress, start a scene or two
(Eliot, "The Love Song of J. Alfred Prufrock")

A more complex example occurs in act five, scene five of *Macbeth*, where the LIFE IS A PLAY metaphor forms the basis of a metonymy. This metonymy has a life itself standing for the person living it. Then, according to the metaphor, a person living a life is an actor in the play:

Life's but a walking shadow, a poor player
That struts and frets his hour upon the stage
And then is heard no more.

Macbeth speaks these lines near the close of the play, when he has lost or wasted all his opportunities for a worthy and meaningful life. Macbeth had many such opportunities. As Thane of Glamis, he was noble and respected. He defeated rebels to King Duncan, and Duncan rewarded him with the title of a rebel thane, the Thane of Cawdor. But Macbeth was ambitious to be king, and in order to become king he killed Duncan (his guest at the time) and arranged the murder of his best friend, Banquo. As a consequence, he lost everything, including the respect of others and the sanity of his wife. Just as a poor player ruins his role by performing badly, so Macbeth ruined his life by misplaying his proper role, trying for a role beyond him. Even a powerfully impressive role can become incoherent and empty in the hands of a bad actor; even a promising and meaningful role in life can become mere strutting and fretting if improperly lived.

LIFE IS BONDAGE; DEATH IS DELIVERANCE

Life can be conceived of in terms of bodily bondage. The soul of the person leading the life is metaphorically a bound prisoner. Being embodied is metaphorically the chain or other physical device that binds the soul. Thus life can be said to imprison the soul in the body, and the body can be said to be a dungeon trapping the soul. The event of death is metaphorically the event of being released from imprisonment, as when the chains break, or as when the prisoner is released from prison.

Death can be personified as someone who frees the prisoner from bondage, via the following interactions. Via LIFE IS BONDAGE, human death is release from physical imprisonment. We have a scenario for such release in which some agent, such as a jailer, performs an action that releases the prisoner from imprisonment. The very fact that people must die—the general phenomenon of death itself—is seen metaphorically as the *cause* of each individual death, and thus as the agent who releases the soul from the body. Thus, death (the general phenomenon) can be personified as the person who breaks the chains or opens the prison door.

LIFE IS BONDAGE underlies Marvell's "Dialogue between the Soul and the Body," in which the soul speaks, complaining of being imprisoned in the body:

> O, who shall from this dungeon raise
> A soul enslaved so many ways?
> With bolts of bones, that fettered stands
> In feet; and manacled in hands.
> Here blinded with an eye: and there
> Deaf with the drumming of an ear;
> A soul hung up, as 'twere, in chains
> Of nerves, and arteries, and veins;
> Tortured, besides each other part,
> In a vain head and double heart?

In these lines, different parts of the body correspond to different kinds of bonds imprisoning the soul in the body. Nerves, arteries, and veins are chains. Feet are fetters. Hands are manacles. And the body as a whole is a dungeon with its various devices for bondage. We know that the prisoner suffers as a result of his imprisonment. Metaphorically, the soul suffers from being imprisoned in a body.

Here is a different passage that focuses not on being bound by life but rather on being delivered by death:

> Then, with no throbs of fiery pain,
> No cold gradations of decay,
> Death broke at once the vital chain,
> And freed his soul the nearest way.
> (Johnson, "Verses on the Death of Mr. Robert
>   Levet")

"Vital" means "having to do with life": vitality itself, life itself, is a chain, and the event of death is the breaking of that chain.

Perhaps the best known use of the life-as-bondage metaphor is Shakespeare's line in Hamlet's soliloquy, "When we have shuffl'd off this mortal coil." The "mortal coil," like the "vital chain," represents the bonds that tie the soul to the body, and shuffling off that coil is the release that death brings.

In the Marvell poem, we saw that the soul was not simply physically bound; it was also *enslaved*, which introduces the additional possibility that life is bondage in servitude rather than physical bondage. We frequently think of servitude as physical bondage, partly because so much servitude actually involves physical bondage, as when slaves are chained or forced to wear a yoke. But we also understand servitude metaphorically in terms of bondage: even domestic slaves in the roles of nanny or butler or cook, who are not afflicted with physical bonds, are nonetheless said to be "under the yoke of slavery" and "placed in chains by their masters." People in servitude throughout the world have often been exhorted to "cast off their chains." Life can therefore be additionally conceived of in terms of the bondage of servitude, as in these examples:

The premeditation of death is the premeditation of
liberty.
He who has learned to die has unlearned to serve.
(Montaigne, *Essays*)

And as by life to bondage man was brought,
Even so likewise by death was freedom wrought.
(John Harington, "Elegy wrote in the Tower, 1554")

LIFE IS A BURDEN

There is a basic metaphor DIFFICULTIES ARE BURDENS,
through which one can comprehend life's difficulties as
"weighing one down" so much that one can "bear" them
only with the "support" of family and friends. This metaphor is coherent with LIFE IS A JOURNEY. Physical burdens
are always difficult, but on a journey they are additionally
impediments to travel, and in the LIFE IS A JOURNEY metaphor, impediments correspond to difficulties in life. If one
further conceives of life as one constant, relentless difficulty,
then it is possible to think of the whole of life as a burden.
Under this view, the condition of being alive is metaphorically the condition of being burdened. This is the basis of a
famous sermon by Donne:

> All our life is a continual burden, yet we must not
> groan; a continual squeezing, yet we must not pant;
> and as in the tenderness of our childhood, we suffer
> and yet are whipped if we cry, so we are complained
> of if we complain, and made delinquents if we call the
> times ill. And that which adds weight to weight and
> multiplies the sadness of this consideration is this: that
> still the best men have the most laid upon them. (Ser-
> mon 66)

At this point, we have seen life and death understood metaphorically in terms of many different concepts—journeys,
plays, days, fluid, plants, sleep, and so on. We have seen
many complicated mappings of knowledge, images, reasoning patterns, properties, and relations. This diversity may
be overwhelming and suggest that anything can be understood metaphorically in terms of anything else, or that all

of our concepts are understood metaphorically in terms of concepts from different domains.

But that is not the case. Although human imagination is strong, empowering us to make and understand even bizarre connections, there are relatively few basic metaphors for life and death that abide as part of our culture. And there are tight constraints on how their mappings work. For example, PEOPLE ARE PLANTS gives us a basis for personifying death as something associated with plants, but not just anything associated with plants will do. The structure of the metaphor exerts strong pressure against any attempt to personify death as an irrigation worker or as the baker who bakes wheat bran into muffins. There are reasons, which we will explore in chapter two, why death the reaper seems apt but death the baker does not.

What is remarkable in what we have seen so far is not how many ways we have of conceiving of life and death, but how few. Where one might expect hundreds of ways of making sense of our most fundamental mysteries, the number of *basic* metaphorical conceptions of life and death turns out to be very small. Though these can be combined and elaborated in novel ways and expressed poetically in an infinity of ways, that infinity is fashioned from the same small set of basic metaphors.

This tells us something important about the nature of creativity. Poets must make the most of the linguistic and conceptual resources they are given. Basic metaphors are part of those conceptual resources, part of the way members of our culture make sense of the world. Poets may compose or elaborate or express them in new ways, but they still use the same basic conceptual resources available to us all. If they did not, we would not understand them.

Shakespearean Complexities

The basic conceptual metaphors that we have discussed so far each give us a different way of comprehending life and death. We have many such perspectives because we need them: we need to be able to conceive of life and death in different ways for different purposes. And the multiplicity of our metaphorical perspectives gives our concepts of life and death a powerful richness. Similarly, one potential source of richness and power in great poetry is the confluence of a number of basic metaphorical perspectives.

Consider Shakespeare's sonnet seventy-three, one of the most exquisite poems in English about death:

> That time of year thou mayst in me behold
> When yellow leaves, or none, or few, do hang
> Upon those boughs which shake against the cold,
> Bare ruined choirs, where late the sweet birds sang.
> In me thou seest the twilight of such day
> As after sunset fadeth in the west;
> Which by and by black night doth take away,
> Death's second self that seals up all in rest.
> In me thou seest the glowing of such fire,
> That on the ashes of his youth doth lie,
> As the deathbed whereon it must expire,
> Consumed with that which it was nourished by.
> This thou perceiv'st, which makes thy love more
>   strong,
> To love that well, which thou must leave ere long.

The first four lines evoke the PEOPLE ARE PLANTS metaphor, in which the stages of life correspond to stages of the plant life cycle. The yellow leaves signal the approach of the end of the cycle, which is old age in the metaphor. The decrepitude of the last stages of old age is set before us by the sequence of images evoked by "none, or few"—first, the tree with all its leaves yellowed, then the defoliated tree with leaves fallen, and finally, and most poignantly, the tree with a few last leaves. It is not merely the leaves, the signs of life, that have gone, but also the singing birds who have taken with them the attributes of spring and summer. This is reinforced by "bare" and "cold," also attributes of late autumn and winter.

The first four lines evoke a superimposition of images. First, "yellow leaves" and "boughs" call up the concept of a tree. The phrase "in me" calls up the concept of a man. One way we connect these is through the conventional PEOPLE ARE PLANTS metaphor, in which people are metaphorically plants with respect to the life cycle. Another way we can connect these is through the superimposition of the image of a tree upon the figure of a man, with limbs corresponding to limbs and trunk to trunk. This possibility is strongly suggested by "boughs which shake against the cold." Trees shake from the wind; and while it might be possible to think of "cold" as suggesting wind, it is usually people who shake from cold. Since the tree is doing what people usually do, the superimposition is immediate and natural.

Second, the expression "bare ruined choirs" describing "boughs" suggests the superimposition of the image of a church choir on the image of a tree, with the ranks of the choir corresponding to the boughs of the tree and the singers to the birds. A major purpose served by this superimposition of the choir loft on the tree, and hence on the man, is to see the man through the choir: as the once intact and song-filled choirs are now ruined and empty, so the once vigorous and vibrant man is now decrepit and diminished.

Whereas the first quatrain characterizes the approach of death via PEOPLE ARE PLANTS and A LIFETIME IS A YEAR, the next two quatrains speak of death using different basic metaphors. The second quatrain begins with A LIFETIME IS A DAY, in which death is night and the twilight after sunset is the stage just before death. The first two lines of the second quatrain are therefore fairly straightforward, but the third and fourth lines of the quatrain raise much more difficult questions:

— What is our metaphorical conception of twilight such that it can be "taken away"?
— How can the taking away be gradual, as suggested by the expression "by and by"?
— By what metaphorical devices is "black night" conceived of as the person who takes twilight away?
— Why is night "death's second self"?
— How can rest be something you can seal something up in? And how can night be doing the sealing?

To answer these questions, we must look simultaneously at the metaphorical conceptions of light, life, death, and night that are active in the passage.

First, light is produced by the sun, which we perceive as moving across the sky and as going away as it sets. Light is therefore understood during daytime as a substance which is present and which gradually "goes away" as the sun sets. Since any change can be conceived of metaphorically as being brought about by a changer, the disappearance of light can be seen as caused by an agent that takes it away.

Second, life is metaphorically conceived of as light, with the span of life corresponding to the daylight hours. In this metaphor, when little daylight remains, little life remains.

Third, life is also metaphorically viewed as a precious possession. Since life is a possession, we can conceive of it as being taken away by an agent.

Thus, we have shown why light can be seen as a substance that can be gradually taken away, and how there can be an agent doing the taking. In addition, we have shown that the agent that takes away light metaphorically corresponds to the agent that takes away life. Let us now turn to the questions: Why is night the agent who takes away light? And why is night "death's second self"?

In the metaphor LIFE IS A PRECIOUS POSSESSION, death is understood as the loss of that possession. If the event of death is understood as an action, it can be seen as the "taking away" of life by some agent. Death itself can be understood as that agent, just as night could be understood as the agent who takes away light. If night takes away light, and death takes away life, and life is light, then it follows that night is "death's second self."

What remains to be answered now are these questions:
— How can night seal something up?
— Why is rest what night seals things up in?
— Why do we understand "rest" in this line as death?
Night is conventionally conceived of metaphorically as a cover, as concealment, as an enclosure. We speak of the cover of night, the cloak of darkness, since, like a cover, the night makes objects inaccessible to vision. Furthermore, to cover something completely is to seal it. One of the principal things we know about death is that the dead person is buried, that is, covered, concealed, enclosed, sealed up. Since, as we have seen, light is life and night is death, the passage is referring to death sealing up "all." Thus, it is being said that just as all things disappear under the cover of night, so all things must die.

At night, typically we go into a state of rest. We have mentioned the metaphor that a state is a location, that is, something we can be *in*. Therefore rest is something that night can seal things up in.

Additionally, there is a basic conceptual metaphor that DEATH IS REST, as we see in "There the wicked cease from troubling; and there the weary be at rest" (Job 3:17). This is reflected in ordinary English in expressions like "going to one's rest."

At this point we should pause to gauge the remarkable complexity of metaphor in these first two quatrains. Here are the basic conceptual metaphors that we have used to make sense of just these first eight lines:

PEOPLE ARE PLANTS
A LIFETIME IS A YEAR
A LIFETIME IS A DAY
LIGHT IS A SUBSTANCE THAT CAN BE TAKEN AWAY
LIFE IS A PRECIOUS POSSESSION
NIGHT IS A COVER
STATES ARE LOCATIONS
DEATH IS REST

The first two were essential in our account of the first four lines, and the next six were essential in our account of the second four lines. The first four lines draw together life as a year and as seasonal cycles of a plant. The second four lines draw together various basic metaphors by which a lifetime is correlated with a day.

The third quatrain draws together various basic metaphors by which life is correlated with a fire. Just as the first two quatrains see the stages of life in terms of the stages of plants and days, so the third quatrain sees the stages of life in terms of the stages of a fire. The life-as-fire metaphor is common throughout English poetry, and Shakespeare makes especially dramatic use of it:

And all our yesterdays have lighted fools
The way to dusty death. Out, out, brief candle!
(*Macbeth* 5.1)

Here the flame of the candle is the flame of life, and because life is conceived of as brief, the candle itself is called brief.

A more elaborate use of LIFE IS A FLAME occurs in act five of Shakespeare's *Othello* when Othello is in the bedroom where Desdemona is asleep. He is contemplating killing her because he suspects her of infidelity. He speaks to a lighted candle:

> Yet she must die, else she'll betray more men.
> Put out the light, and then put out the light:
> If I quench thee, thou flaming minister,
> I can again thy former light restore,
> Should I repent me; but once put out thy light,
> Thou cunning'st pattern of excelling nature,
> I know not where is that Promethean heat
> That can thy light relume.

Othello explicitly differentiates the flame of the candle from the flame of her life: he can put out the candle as he can snuff out her life, but it is only the candle that he can relight.

In the third quatrain of sonnet seventy-three, Shakespeare makes use of our knowledge of the stages of a fire: the early flaming up is the heat of youth; the steady flame is middle age; the embers glowing among the ashes are old age; and the cold ashes are death.

> In me thou seest the glowing of such fire,
> That on the ashes of his youth doth lie,
> As the deathbed whereon it must expire,
> Consumed with that which it was nourished by.

The "glowing" in the first line suggests that the speaker is old. But now several questions arise:
— What are "the ashes of his youth"?
— What does it mean that he is "lying" on them?
— Why are these ashes a deathbed?
    How do we make sense of the notion that the fire of life is consumed with what once nourished it?

To answer these questions, we need to consider our conventional image of what a fire looks like, together with nonimagistic knowledge about fires associated with that image. We know that each fire has only so much wood to burn, and once burned it becomes ashes and cannot burn again. For a fire to burn steadily, it must burn very hot in its early stages.

This requires that it consume a lot of fuel early. As fuel is consumed, it becomes ashes, which are both the residue of the fuel and the result of the burning. As a fire burns down, the ashes settle to the bottom. At the fire's end, the ashes are on the ground and the embers in the ashes. As the fire dies, the ashes help smother the embers.

We use all of this knowledge about the course of the burning of a fire to make sense of this passage. The life-as-fire metaphor guides us in connecting our knowledge of fires to our conception of a human lifetime. In the life-as-fire metaphor, the wood corresponds to the energy available to us in living our lives. The early stage of the fire corresponds to youth. The ashes correspond to the consequences of earlier living. The ashes are also evidence of having used up a measure of our allotted energy. The early hot burning corresponds to the vigor of youth. The embers correspond to the diminished vitality of old age. And the bed of ashes corresponds to the consequences of one's earlier life that surround one in old age.

How can we make sense of "ashes of his youth"? They are the residue of the speaker's earlier life, the consequences that he must now deal with. The ashes are also evidence of a diminished vitality.

It now becomes clear what "lying" and "deathbed" refer to. "The glowing of such fire" together with "lying on the ashes" evokes the image of embers. Imagistically, just as the embers lie on the ashes, so a person near death lies on his deathbed. The life-as-fire metaphor at this point gives rise to the following inferences: the speaker presents himself as old and near death, surrounded by the consequences of his earlier life, active at a much lower level, his vitality diminished forever like a fire that can never roar again.

Let us now turn to the question of how we make sense of "consumed with that which it was nourished by." First, we need to explain how the fire of life can be "consumed." Just as the ashes help smother the last embers of a fire, so the speaker sees the residue of his earlier life as diminishing him even further in old age. There is an irony here. The ashes are two things: that which smothers the embers and that which is left over of the wood. Thus, what ultimately consumes his life is what once fed, or "nourished," the fires of youth.

So far, we have been discussing each quatrain as if it were a separate poem. But the metaphors in the three quatrains are supplementary and reinforcing; that is why they are all in this one poem. They all talk about a near-final stage within a succession of life stages. And they all characterize this near-final stage in terms of a poignant diminishment of intensity. Each quatrain thus provides a different metaphorical take on the same scene. And the power of the poem resides in large measure in the relentlessness of the characterization, whatever the metaphor.

It should be clear at this point that an understanding of the metaphors in this poem is a prerequisite to any serious understanding of the poem. But we are not suggesting that to understand the metaphors is to understand the poem. Sonnet seventy-three is a striking example of this fact. Though the metaphors in the poem suggest that the speaker is near death, there are other aspects of the poem that can be taken as suggesting that he is not. For example, take the phrases "thou mayst in me behold," "in me thou seest," and "this thou perceiv'st." It is strange to tell someone you are talking to what it is that they see. To say that someone, presumably someone who knows you very well, *may* perceive something as obvious as advanced old age in you suggests that the perception is inaccurate or that the speaker is exaggerating.

Or one might assume that the speaker in this sonnet is also the speaker in other sonnets in the sequence of which this sonnet is one small part and that they all concern roughly the same stage of the speaker's life. On the basis of the other sonnets, we might be led to believe that the speaker does not conceive of himself as old at all. Thus, we might take the speaker as exaggerating and speculate on his motives. Perhaps he is insecure; perhaps he is trying to evoke reassurance; perhaps—as the line "which makes thy love more strong" suggests—he is trying to influence the feelings of the the person he is addressing. Before one can even ask such questions or make such speculations, one must understand the basic metaphorical structure of the poem.

Such complexity of metaphors about life and death is not unusual in poems we find compelling. We might have given a similar analysis of Dylan Thomas's "Do Not Go Gentle into that Good Night." Here, too, we would find instances of the basic metaphors of a lifetime as a day and death as night, of life as fire and a journey, and of death as departure and as an adversary.

> Do not go gentle into that good night,
> Old age should burn and rave at close of day;
> Rage, rage against the dying of the light.
>
> Though wise men at their end know dark is right,
> Because their words had forked no lightning they
> Do not go gentle into that good night.
>
> Good men, the last wave by, crying how bright
> Their frail deeds might have danced in a green bay,
> Rage, rage against the dying of the light.
>
> Wild men who caught and sang the sun in flight,
> And learn, too late, they grieved it on its way,
> Do not go gentle into that good night.
>
> Grave men, near death, who see with blinding sight
> Blind eyes could blaze like meteors and be gay,
> Rage, rage against the dying of the light.
>
> And you, my father, there on the sad height,
> Curse, bless, me now with your fierce tears, I pray.
> Do not go gentle into that good night.
> Rage, rage against the dying of the light.

Time

Our understanding of life and death is very much bound up with our understanding of time. This is because death is inevitable and because the mere passage of time can be seen as bringing about inevitable events. Hence, in the case of inevitable events, time can be seen as playing a causal role. When we say "it is just a matter of time" about some potential occurrence, we mean that the passage of time will inevitably bring the event to transpire. One of our major cultural models of life is that each of us is allotted a certain fixed time on earth. Our allotted time will eventually be used up, and we will die. It is no accident that two of the major metaphors for death that we have seen involve spans of time: a day and a year. In fact, two of the examples we cited above as being about death actually mention only time.

> . . . what inexorable cause
> Makes Time so vicious in his reaping.
> (Robinson, "For a Dead Lady")

> But, at my back I always hear
> Time's wingèd chariot hurrying near
> (Marvell, "To His Coy Mistress")

TIME IS A THIEF

It seems clear that no full understanding of the metaphors for life and death is possible without an understanding of how they relate to our conceptions of time. For example, Milton reflects on his mortality by using a metaphor for time:

> How soon hath Time, the subtle thief of youth,
> Stolen on his wing my three and twentieth year!
> (Sonnet 7)

Such a remark on the brevity of life and the speed of its passage indirectly calls up the spectre of old age and its infirmities. Virgil expresses the same sentiment in:

> Time bears away all things, even the mind.
> (*Eclogues*, 9)

We comprehend such passages immediately and with little or no effort. However, a close inspection of Milton's lines reveals a remarkable complexity whose nature is anything but immediately clear:
— How can time be an agent, in particular, a person?
— How can time be the kind of person who steals?
— How can a year of our life, or our youth as a whole, be things that can be stolen?
— How do we make sense of the expression "subtle thief"? Why "subtle"?
— Why does time have wings?
— How does this collection of metaphors communicate what it does?

35

To make sense of these lines from Milton, we make use of a conception of life as a precious possession. This life-as-a-possession metaphor can be seen in such expressions as "He lost his life in an accident," "I regret that I have but one life to give for my country," and "My life is my own." Or, as A. E. Houseman puts it,

> Now, of my threescore years and ten,
> Twenty will not come again.
> And take from seventy springs a score,
> That only leaves me fifty more.

As we see in these lines, it is not just our whole life that is conceived of as a possession, but portions of it as well, for example a score of years or even an individual year. Thus we understand "my three and twentieth year" in the Milton passage as a possession, which is why it can be "stolen."

In addition to possessing all the portions of one's life, one also characteristically possesses at various times certain properties, such as beauty, strength, and youth. Because youth is a possession, it too can be stolen, and hence the phrase "thief of youth."

This explains how a year and one's youth can be possessions and therefore how they can be stolen; but it does not explain why time can be an agent who does the stealing. As we live our lives, less and less of the allotted time remains and various properties such as beauty or youth diminish or disappear. The disappearances of these properties are events. A noteworthy event is commonly understood not as just happening but as being caused by some agent and thus as being the consequence of an action. A huge proportion of the events that happen to us are, indeed, caused by agents, as when the vase falls off the table and we note that the cat knocked it over. And events that need not be thought of as caused by agents are often understood as if they are. For instance, we often make sense of natural events by ascribing some agency to an aspect of nature, as when we speak of the wind as knocking over a tree and killing the person in the car underneath it.

In addition, we very commonly conceive of agentless events metaphorically as if they were caused by agents:

The boulder resisted all of our efforts to move it.
Events conspired to delay the game.
The computer wiped out my buffer.
The computer spewed garbage at me.
My car just refused to start this morning.

Such cases are all instances of a very general EVENTS ARE
ACTIONS metaphor, which imputes agency to something
causally connected to the event. As we saw in "black night
doth take away," such metaphorical agents frequently are
taken to have human qualities.

In our understanding of events, frequently we ascribe the
occurrence of a particular event to a nonincidental property of something indispensably involved in the event. This
means that we are finding a significant causal link between
the occurrence and the property. Then, using EVENTS ARE
ACTIONS, we can personify the possessor of that property
as the actor who causes the event. For example, it is a nonincidental property of time that it inevitably passes. When
we ascribe the occurrence of a particular event to the passage of time, we can therefore personify time as an actor
playing a causal role in the occurrence of that event.

At this point, we can see that:

— Life, portions of life, and properties such as beauty and
youth cease to exist in the passage of time.
— Time inevitably passes. Therefore, life, portions of life,
and properties such as beauty and youth inevitably cease
to exist.
— The passage of time is seen as playing a causal role in
these events.
— Time can thus be seen as a metaphorical agent, and the
event as an action by that agent.
— Because life and portions of life are possessions, their
disappearances are losses, and the agent of loss can be a
thief.

But Milton does not just say that there is some thief or
other; he specifies time as the thief and in doing so provides
us with a way of understanding time. In specifying time as
the thief, he is personifying time, that is, inviting us to understand the principles by which time operates in terms of
the characteristics of a thief. Just as thieves take valuable

possessions of ours forever, so when time robs us of a year or our youth, it is also taking a valuable possession forever. Just as theft leaves one with a feeling of helplessness over the loss of something irreplaceable, so we are helpless before the passage of time.

Thus there is a difference between the mere attribution of some agency and the identification of a particular agent. The creation of an agent is a consequence of the EVENTS ARE ACTIONS metaphor, but the choice of a particular entity to which to ascribe such agency is a separate process of personification—a process which results from the fact that humans are readily identifiable as agents of specific kinds. One might express an event as an action without identifying the agent, as one does with a passive sentence like "My youth has been stolen from me," which involves no personification at all.

By contrast, consider:

> Time has stolen my youth.
> Work has stolen my youth.
> Education has stolen my youth.

Each of these sentences describes the passage of youth as an action undertaken by a particular agent—here the agent is a thief—by virtue of personifying something abstract. But while each abstract entity is portrayed as the same kind of agent, what is being personified is different in each case, and hence the sentences are about different subject matters.

At this point there are three questions that must be answered:

— How is it that a personification can communicate something about a subject matter such as time or education?
— What is it that the personification of time as a thief communicates?
— What constraints are there on the personification mapping?

A personification is a metaphor. As such it has a source domain, in this case theft, and a target domain, in this case time. We use a metaphor to map certain aspects of the source domain onto the target domain, thereby producing a new understanding of that target domain. In this case, part of that mapping superimposes a metaphorical understanding of youth as a possession, which carries with it our normal feelings about possessions—that we have a right to keep them and that it would be unjust for them to be taken away.

It imposes some properties on time on which we can base certain understandings and concomitant evaluations: that, in being an agent of an action that harms us, time is dishonest and malicious. It also highlights the lack of control over the loss of youth. At the same time, anything that contradicts this view is hidden: in particular, the metaphor of time as a thief hides the idea that it is a matter of natural law that everything gets old and dies, and that therefore no one has a right not to.

But the fact that any metaphor highlights some aspects of an event and hides others does not mean that just any view can be imposed on time, or any target domain, with equal ease. One cannot personify time as just any random agent and leave it at that. Rather, for the metaphor to work, we must find—or impose—some correspondence between the ways that a particular agent acts and our knowledge of the kinds of events typical of the target domain. In this case, we have a great deal of knowledge about time, independent of any personification: at any moment, there is a certain portion of life remaining to us and another portion that we have lived and no longer have. What we have of life gradually becomes what we no longer have. Thus, it is natural from this perspective to personify time as a thief, who takes something we have and makes it into something we don't have.

We are now in a position to explain why this thief is subtle. Usually when a thief steals something, first we have it entirely and then it is entirely gone and we really notice the change. But this thief, like a real-world thief who gradually drains a bank account, steals little by little—subtly—so that we may not notice for a while. This explains the words "How soon?" The speaker is not surprised that years and youth gradually go away. Rather he is surprised at how subtly so much of it is already gone without his noticing. This realization speaks to us all. The allotted span of life remaining is always diminishing for us. But, caught up in living our lives, we may not notice this until we find ourselves surprised and then thoughtful at how much has gone by.

We are finally in a position to answer the last question in our list: why is Time, the thief, winged in this poem? The answer seems obvious: because time flies. But what does it mean that time flies? First, time is often understood metaphorically as a moving object, as in sentences like "The time for action has arrived" or "That time has long since gone." Time is moving in this poem, flying as opposed to creeping, because the poem is about how quickly time passes and about how hard it is to notice that it is going by.

THE GENERAL CASE: TIME IS A CHANGER

The TIME IS A THIEF metaphor concerns change of a certain kind, the barely noticeable passing of time and, with it, the loss of youth. Many kinds of things change with time: values, landscapes, objects, personal appearance, and so on. Moreover, things change in many ways: they can be transformed, they can grow, they can be destroyed, or they can just disappear. Because changes are events, they can be understood via the EVENTS ARE ACTIONS metaphor as acts on the part of an agent who is effecting the change. Because changes occur as time passes, it is possible to personify time itself as being the agent of change, that is, to see time generally as a changer. But what kind of changer time is will depend on what is changing, how it is changing, and how we conceive of that change by still other metaphors.

In the previous section, we saw a special case of time as changer, where the change was the loss of a metaphorical possession, youth. We saw that the TIME IS A THIEF metaphor is a composite of the general TIME IS A CHANGER metaphor plus the LIFE IS A POSSESSION metaphor. We will now turn to a variety of other special cases where the general TIME IS A CHANGER metaphor applies. What will differentiate these cases will be the additional information, which may be metaphorical or not, that characterizes the nature and object of the change.

40

TIME IS A REAPER

The additional knowledge-structuring that characterizes the change in the time-as-a-reaper metaphor is metaphorical: it comes from the basic metaphor PEOPLE ARE PLANTS, one aspect of which is that PROPERTIES OF PEOPLE ARE PLANT PARTS. Thus, the Robinson passage cited above, "what inexorable cause / Makes Time so vicious in his reaping," can be understood in two ways in terms of this basic metaphor. If it is the whole plant that time is cutting down (as with wheat, for example), then the passage is about death, since the reaping of the whole plant is the death of the person. If it is merely parts of the plant that time is reaping (as in plucking flowers, picking fruits, and so on), then the passage is about the disappearance of certain properties of a person, such as youth, beauty, or mental acuity, as in "Beauty is but a flower" (Thomas Nashe). This shows not only that we can arrive at alternative readings of a passage by bringing to bear different basic metaphors but also that we can arrive at alternative readings by bringing to bear different parts of the same basic metaphor.

The metaphorical idea that time can reap parts of plants as well as the whole plant is fairly common in Western poetry, as in this passage from Shakespeare's sonnet 116:

> Love's not Time's fool, though rosy lips and cheeks
> Within his bending sickle's compass come.

The rosy lips and cheeks, by metonymy, stand for youthful beauty, which disappears in time.

TIME IS A DEVOURER

We have seen that the metaphors for time as a thief and as a reaper result from the basic TIME IS A CHANGER metaphor plus some additional structured knowledge that comes from the independently existing metaphors LIFE IS A POSSESSION and PEOPLE ARE PLANTS. In the next three special cases of TIME IS A CHANGER, the information that yields the special cases comes from commonplace notions, not metaphors.

Going out of existence over time is an event of change. This type of change may be expressed metaphorically if time is seen as an agent who brings about the sorts of change involved. One kind of agent that qualifies is a devourer. This is because of our commonplace notion that things that are eaten go out of existence. While we all know that things eaten are biologically transformed into energy and waste, those things also lose their integrity as objects and become imperceptible to us. This underlies the notion that they cease to exist. Moreover, our commonsense knowledge that we eat food gradually in bite-sized portions coheres with our sense of the gradual passing of our youth, and the violence associated with biting and chewing reinforces the evaluation of time as a malicious taker of youth.

So Ovid can say "Time, the devourer of everything" (*Metamorphoses* 15). In sonnet nineteen, Shakespeare refers to "devouring time," and in *The Rape of Lucrece* he refers to time as the "eater of youth." A particular kind of devourer is a predator, a beast that kills you and then eats you. Calling upon the knowledge that a cormorant is a rapacious water bird that preys on fish, Shakespeare in *Love's Labor's Lost* 1.1 refers to "cormorant devouring time."

TIME IS A DESTROYER

Falling apart is another kind of change. An agent who makes things fall apart is a destroyer. So time can be a destroyer, as in:

> Does it really exist, Time, the destroyer?
> When will it crush the fortress on the peaceful
>   height?
> (Rainer Maria Rilke, *Sonnets to Orpheus*, 2)

TIME IS AN EVALUATOR

Another form of change is change of value. Since time is a changer, time can be viewed as the agent that reassesses values we place on things. Any metaphor that personifies time in this way must conform to our knowledge about how values are changed. One way is that false judgments can be corrected. Another is that true ones can be validated. So we say that things pass or fail the judgment of time. And Byron can say, in *Childe Harold's Pilgrimage*,

> Time! the Correcter where our judgments err.

Since our laws embody our values, legal changes typically reflect changes in values. Time can thus be seen as H. L. Mencken saw it:

> Time is a great legalizer, even in the field of morals.

Other ways to change values are to pardon and to honor. So Auden can write:

> Time that is intolerant
> Of the brave and innocent,
> And indifferent in a week
> To a beautiful physique,
> Worships language and forgives
> Everyone by whom it lives;
> Pardons cowardice, conceit,
> Lays its honors at their feet.
> Time that with this strange excuse
> Pardoned Kipling and his views,
> And will pardon Paul Claudel,
> Pardons him for writing well.
> ("In Memory of W. B. Yeats")

Thus, when we view time as a thief, a reaper, a devourer, a destroyer, or an evaluator, we are viewing time generally as a changer and adding further information to characterize the nature of the change. There are many such special cases of the time-as-a-changer metaphor, too many to list. To get a sense of the variety, consider cases like "Time heals all wounds," "Time has carved the face of the canyon," "Time etched wrinkles in his brow," and "Time is the rider that breaks youth." Since things heal over time, we can personify time as the healer, and so on. All such special cases arise from using additional information to characterize the nature of the change and from our ability to find the right kind of agent.

Let us now turn to another conception of time, where time is not viewed as a changer.

Time Moves

Consider these lines from act one, scene three of *Macbeth*:

> Come what come may
> Time and the hour runs through the roughest day

In this case, time is seen as running, as moving in the direction of the future, that is, as propelling itself. This is a combination of the EVENTS ARE ACTIONS metaphor, where time is the actor, with a metaphorical way of understanding temporal change in terms of motion—the metaphor that TIME MOVES. In the version found here, the present moment is seen as moving forward in the direction of the future. Time can thus be a runner, since a runner is both moving and the actor responsible for the movement. What we know about runners thus simultaneously fits the combination of EVENTS ARE ACTIONS and TIME MOVES and adds the attribute of swiftness to the motion of time.

The TIME MOVES metaphor has two versions: in both, we are located at the present and are facing toward the future with the past at our back. The views differ on whether it is the future that is moving toward us, or whether we, at the present moment, are moving toward it. In the most conventionalized view, we are stationary and moments of time move by us, approaching us from the future and going away from us into the past. Thus, we say "The deadline is approaching," "That time will come soon enough," "That time is long gone," and so on. Just as we are facing toward the future, the future times are facing us as they approach us. Thus we speak of "the face of things to come" and "facing the future." Consequently, when times are considered relative not to us but rather to other times, we use words like "precede" and "follow," and "before" and "after," in accordance with the orientation of the times as having their faces to their pasts (what precedes them) and their backs to their futures (what follows them). Thus, today is the day preceding tomorrow, and the day following tomorrow is two days from now.

In the other view, the past and future are fixed and the

present is in motion toward the future. There are two versions of this view. In one, we are always located at the present and we move toward scheduled future events, as in "We're coming up on our twentieth wedding anniversary," "We're approaching blast-off," and "We're nearing the runoff election." Alternatively, the present time itself can be seen as a point moving toward future points in scheduled time, as in "The hour is approaching midnight," and "It's getting close to bedtime."

From the point of view of our everyday experience, it is clear why both versions should be available to us: sometimes we move toward objects and sometimes they move toward us. Moreover, the sun, which is a natural model for analog clocks, moves along a fixed path, and its location on that path determines the present moment. Thus, the sun, as the present moment, is always moving toward foreseeable future moments. It is clear that both versions of the metaphor of time as moving are natural, relative to two different kinds of normal experience.

By virtue of the second view of time (the present moving toward the future), we can explain metaphoric expressions such as "We're racing against time to finish the assignment" and "We're trying to beat the clock." In such expressions, our purposes are destinations, and we are moving on the path toward accomplishing them. Simultaneously, the present is on its path moving toward the point in time by which the purpose must be accomplished. Our desire is to arrive at our destination, the accomplishment of our purpose, before the present moment arrives at the deadline. Thus, there are two metaphoric paths here: a purposive path and a time path. They are oriented in the same direction: the direction from us to our goals is the same as the direction from the present to the future (since we are in the present and our goals are in the future). Moreover, there is something moving along each path—we toward our purposes, and the present time toward the future. Thus, the two runners (us and the present time) are headed in the same direction along parallel paths. This makes it easy to conceive of the situation as a foot race between us and an opponent (the present time), who is running in the same direction as we are, along a parallel path. We win the race against time if we achieve the goal before the deadline, that is, before the present time reaches the time at which the goal must be accomplished.

As we have seen, the race against time involves the concept of a deadline, a scheduled or expected time for achieving a given purpose. In addition to a deadline, there can also be a schedule of expected progress. Thus, one can speak of being "ahead of time." What this means is that where we are on the path of accomplishment toward our goal is *ahead of* where we were scheduled to be by the present time. When we say "*We* are ahead of *time*," we are using two metonymies: *we* stands for the point that we are at on the path from past to future events, and *time* stands for the point on that path at which we were scheduled to be at the present time.

TIME IS A PURSUER

One of the major metaphorical links between time and death is a composite of EVENTS ARE ACTIONS, TIME MOVES, and LIFE IS A JOURNEY. As we move along life's path trying to achieve our goals in life (which are metaphorically destinations on the path), we are racing against time. When time catches up to us, it stops us and we die: we can no longer reach any future events:

> But at my back I always hear
> Time's wingèd chariot hurrying near.
> (Marvell, "To His Coy Mistress")

> Time overtakes all things alike.
> (Aeschylus, *Eumenides*)

The nature of death as conceived of in this metaphor is that it is something you want to avoid and that you take action to avoid, ultimately in vain. The actions of a pursuer who will ultimately catch you conform to this characterization of death. The pursuer is unwanted. You can try to avoid him by running away. Running takes extra effort. And the pursuer is someone you cannot outrun.

Time Hath a Wallet

We have just listed a number of basic metaphors for time, ways of conceptualizing time that recur throughout the body of Western poetry. As we saw in the case of death metaphors, it is possible for basic metaphors to combine in a given passage to yield a new complex metaphor. This is equally true of the conventional basic metaphors for time, as we will now demonstrate.

The following passage from act three, scene three of Shakespeare's *Troilus and Cressida* is spoken by Ulysses to Achilles during the Trojan War. Achilles, previously renowned for his deeds in the war, has been insulted by Agamemnon and has withdrawn indefinitely from the fight. In hopes of getting him to return to the battle, Ulysses has staged several scenes in which Ajax is praised and Achilles is brushed aside. Achilles wonders why no one pays him his due respect any more, and Ulysses explains that good deeds are soon forgotten:

> Time hath, my lord, a wallet at his back,
> Wherein he puts alms for Oblivion,
> A great-siz'd monster of ingratitudes.
> Those scraps are good deeds past, which are devour'd
> As fast as they are made, forgot as soon
> As done.

There are a number of questions that arise naturally about such a passage, and we are now in a position to answer them:
— Why is time personified?
— Why does he have a wallet?
— Why is he putting things in it?
— Although there is no mention of time moving in the passage, most readers will understand that time is moving, and in particular walking. Why is that?
— Is Time facing toward the past or the future, or neither?
— Why is the wallet at his back?
— How do we understand the relationship between Oblivion and Time?
— How can we understand Oblivion as a "monster of ingratitude"?

— How can we understand Oblivion as "devouring"?

— Why is it that what Oblivion devours is "good deeds past"?

— Why are the things Time puts in the wallet called "alms" instead of any of the infinity of other things they could be called?

The passage refers to a situation where Achilles' good deeds have been forgotten. Because forgetting is an event of change over time, we can employ the EVENTS ARE ACTIONS metaphor to view an event as the result of an action by an agent. Since the change is seen as caused by the passage of time, the TIME IS A CHANGER metaphor is applicable and appropriate. By this means, time becomes personified as the agent of change.

Next we need to address several questions. Why does Time have a wallet (that is, a pouch, which is what "wallet" referred to in Shakespeare's time)? Why is the wallet at his back? And why is he putting things into it? When something is forgotten, it ceases to be something in one's conscious awareness, or in metaphorical terms, it is removed from "mental sight." Mental sight is relevant here since conscious knowledge is commonly understood via the KNOWING IS SEEING metaphor, as in sentences like "I see what you're getting at." Putting EVENTS ARE ACTIONS, TIME IS A CHANGER, and KNOWING IS SEEING together, we arrive at a conception of time as making things disappear from sight and thus become forgotten. This explains why Time puts things into a wallet, which is closed and dark and therefore hides them. It also provides part of the reason why the wallet is at his back, because it is then inaccessible to his vision.

Most readers appear to understand Time in this passage as moving, even though nothing about that is said in the passage. Given that we ordinarily understand time as moving, this is natural. We can also explain in which direction it must be moving. If Time is the moving present, the future must be ahead and the past behind. This explains why the wallet is at his back: since the past is at his back and the wallet contains past deeds, the wallet must be at his back. So the wallet at his back coheres both with the conception of time as a moving object and with the conception of knowing as seeing.

Let us now turn to the role of Oblivion in the passage. Oblivion is the state of being permanently forgotten. States are generally understood metaphorically as locations, that is, something one is "in." Going into oblivion is therefore a permanent change to an inaccessible location. As a change, it is an event, and as an event, it can be understood via EVENTS ARE ACTIONS as an act by an agent. A devourer is a suitable metaphorical agent because once something is devoured it is in a permanently inaccessible location.

So far we have seen that Time is viewed as an agent who collects things and then hands them over to Oblivion to devour. Let us now consider why Oblivion is viewed as a "monster of ingratitude." Oblivion, in the passage, is personified as the agent who causes Achilles' good deeds to be forgotten forever by those for whom they were done. Such a forgetting of good deeds done for one's benefit is ingratitude, which we feel to be repugnant and monstrous. In order to express such feelings, the author must characterize Oblivion as something toward whom we have the same feelings—a monster. As Shakespeare says in *King Lear* 1.2, "Ingratitude, thou marble-hearted fiend."

Finally, we need to explain why good deeds past are "alms" for Oblivion. Ulysses, in this passage, wants to convey a sense of the ease and speed with which good deeds past become forgotten. So those deeds must be small and insignificant to the agent who is disposing of them. So these good deeds are called "alms," that is, small things so insignificant they can be given to beggars. Thus it is very natural for us to get an image in which the alms are small in size relative to both Time and Oblivion.

Thus, this complex of metaphors coheres to convey to Achilles how easily his renown can be forgotten, and therefore how persistently he must work at maintaining it.

Conclusion

In the "Time hath a wallet" passage, as in all the examples that we have examined in this chapter, the basic conceptual metaphors used to understand a metaphorical text are not just in the words. Metaphorical understanding is not a matter of mere word play; it is endemically conceptual in nature. It is indispensable to comprehending and reasoning about concepts like life, death, and time.

It is a prerequisite to any discussion of metaphor that we make a distinction between basic conceptual metaphors, which are cognitive in nature, and particular linguistic expressions of these conceptual metaphors. Thus, though a particular poetic passage may give a unique linguistic expression of a basic metaphor, the conceptual metaphor underlying it may nonetheless be extremely common. The Shakespearean sonnet that we discussed at length is unique nearly to the point of immortality, but the conceptual metaphors underlying it are some of the most common in Western thought and recur in poem after poem, as we have seen.

Any discussion of the uniqueness or idiosyncrasy of a metaphor must therefore take place on two levels: the conceptual level and the linguistic level. A given passage may express a common conceptual metaphor in a way that is linguistically either commonplace or idiosyncratic. An idiosyncratic conceptual metaphor is another matter. By its very nature, it cannot yet be deeply conventionalized in our thought, and therefore its linguistic expression will necessarily be idiosyncratic in at least some respect. Modes of thought that are not themselves conventional cannot be expressed in conventional language. In short, idiosyncrasy of language may or may not express idiosyncrasy of thought, but idiosyncratic thought requires idiosyncratic language.

At both the conceptual and linguistic levels, we have the resources to construct an indefinitely large range of metaphors, that is, metaphorical concepts and ways of expressing such concepts in language. Given any well-structured concept, an inventive person can probably find a way to understand another concept using it. For example, we could probably all find some way or other to make sense of "Death is a banana," that is, to understand the concept of death in terms of what we know about bananas. There are important differences between such a random, idiosyn-

cratic conceptualization of death and so basic a metaphor as
DEATH IS DEPARTURE.

Basic conceptual metaphors are part of the common conceptual apparatus shared by members of a culture. They are
systematic in that there is a fixed correspondence between
the structure of the domain to be understood (e.g., death)
and the structure of the domain in terms of which we are
understanding it (e.g., departure). We usually understand
them in terms of common experiences. They are largely unconscious, though attention may be drawn to them. Their
operation in cognition is mostly automatic. And they are
widely conventionalized in language, that is, there are a
great number of words and idiomatic expressions in our
language whose interpretations depend upon those conceptual metaphors. But there are no words or idiomatic expressions in our language whose meanings depend upon a
conceptual connection between death and a banana.

Thus we see that though there is an infinitude of potential conceptual metaphors, only a very few of these have
special status as basic metaphors in our conceptual systems.
It is also the case that there is an infinitude of potential
metaphorical expressions at the linguistic level, but this
does not imply that they are all conceptually unique. The
reason is that the relatively small number of basic conceptual metaphors can be combined conceptually and expressed in an infinite variety of linguistic expressions.

With respect to the relatively small number of existing
basic metaphors at the conceptual level, there are three
stances that poets have chosen to take toward them. The
first is simply to versify them in automatic ways; this results
in a lot of lame, feeble, and trite verse. The second is to
deploy them masterfully, combining them, extending them,
and crystallizing them in strong images, as we saw in the
lengthy quotations from Shakespeare and Dylan Thomas.
The third stance is to attempt to step outside the ordinary
ways we think metaphorically and either to offer new modes
of metaphorical thought or to make the use of our conventional basic metaphors less automatic by employing them in
unusual ways, or otherwise to destabilize them and thus

51

reveal their inadequacies for making sense of reality. The third stance is part of what characterizes the avant-garde in any age.

Metaphor isn't just for poets; it's in ordinary language and is the principal way we have of conceptualizing abstract concepts like life, death, and time. Let us look at the list of basic conceptual metaphors that we have encountered in this chapter:

Very General Metaphors

> PURPOSES ARE DESTINATIONS
> STATES ARE LOCATIONS
> EVENTS ARE ACTIONS

Metaphors for Time

> TIME IS A CHANGER
> TIME MOVES
> TIME IS A PURSUER

Metaphors for Life and Death

> LIFE IS A JOURNEY
> DEATH IS DEPARTURE
> PEOPLE ARE PLANTS
> A LIFETIME IS A YEAR
> A LIFETIME IS A DAY
> DEATH IS SLEEP
> DEATH IS REST
> LIFE IS A PRECIOUS POSSESSION
> LIFE IS A PLAY
> LIFE IS A FLAME
> LIFE IS A FIRE
> LIFE IS A FLUID
> LIFE IS BONDAGE
> LIFE IS A BURDEN

The reason why there are so many conventional metaphors for life, death, and time is that these are very rich concepts for us. When we try to conceptualize the wealth of our experiences of these domains, no single, consistent structuring of that experience is possible; instead we need to import structure from a wide variety of source domains if we are to characterize anything approaching the full richness of the target domains. Each metaphor provides structure for comprehending a different aspect of the target domain. Thus LIFE IS A PRECIOUS POSSESSION makes sense for us of a different aspect of life than does LIFE IS A JOURNEY or LIFE IS BONDAGE. Because different metaphors for life are about different aspects of life, it is not surprising that source-domain structures used for understanding them are often inconsistent. For example, LIFE IS A PRECIOUS POSSESSION and LIFE IS BONDAGE provide very different perspectives on life.

Most of these basic conceptual metaphors that we found to underlie poetic examples also underlie everyday expressions. We have seen this already for DEATH IS DEPARTURE, PURPOSES ARE DESTINATIONS, and EVENTS ARE ACTIONS. Even the basic metaphors in this list that seem to us to be strikingly poetic are conventionalized in everyday language. We have seen that the metaphor LIFE IS A PLAY, which underlies poetic metaphors like "All the world's a stage," appears as well in a plethora of everyday expressions.

The basic metaphor that TIME MOVES, while underlying immortal poetic metaphors like "To-morrow, and to-morrow, and to-morrow, / Creeps in this petty pace from day after day," also underlies everyday proverbs like "Time waits for no man." It additionally underlies the most normal of expressions, such as "The deadline is approaching" and "Sunday will be here soon enough." And the same PEOPLE ARE PLANTS metaphor used in Shakespeare's sonnet seventy-three and Lear's expression "Ripeness is all" is also the basis for everyday expressions like "She's in the full flower of youth," "She's a late bloomer," "He's withering," and "She's a budding beauty." Because basic metaphors occur at the conceptual level, they can be either conventionalized in everyday language or pushed beyond the conventional into poetic uses.

This raises a question: if we often have the same conceptual metaphors in ordinary language as in poetry, why is it that the poetry should seem so much harder? There are a number of reasons. First, poetic uses are often conscious extensions of the ordinary conventionalized metaphors; for

example, "Time hath a wallet" is in part an extension of
TIME MOVES. Because they are conscious, they can draw
upon different cognitive resources than the automatic and
effortless use of fully conventionalized modes of metaphorical expression. Second, authors may call upon our knowledge of basic conceptual metaphors in order to manipulate
them in unusual ways. The unusual use of a normally automatic and unconscious metaphor takes effort. In his sonnet
seventy-three, for example, in speaking of life as a fire which
is "consumed by that which it was nourished by," Shakespeare is taking an unusual perspective on an ordinary
metaphor.

Third, in everyday language, it is unusual to find two or
more basic metaphors for the same target domain in a single
clause, although one may find them in adjacent clauses. To
illustrate the difference between poetic compression and
periphrastic prolixity, contrast the Shakespeare passage with
a paraphrase:

> Time hath, my lord, a wallet at his back,
> Wherein he puts alms for Oblivion,
> A great-siz'd monster of ingratitudes.
> Those scraps are good deeds past, which are devour'd
> As fast as they are made, forgot as soon
> As done.

> Our good deeds are things we leave behind us that
> we like to look at and admire, and have other
> people look at and admire. But Time, as it moves
> forward, picks up our good deeds, which are
> insignificant relative to Time itself, and Time puts
> them where no one can see them, and then later
> gives them as scraps to Oblivion, which is a hungry
> monster who devours them so that they will never
> be seen again.

This is a paraphrase that preserves most of the basic conceptual metaphors in the Shakespeare passage but distributes
them over many clauses. The basic metaphors are not creations of poets; rather, it is the masterful way in which poets
extend, compose, and compress them that we find poetic.

Poetic compression accounts in part for the effort required to comprehend rich poetry, even when all the metaphors in it are basic metaphors.

Fourth, poetry may be complex for reasons independent of the use of metaphors. It may be phonologically or syntactically or otherwise complex or unusual. For these reasons, a poem may be difficult to interpret and hard to process even though it uses only the most common basic conceptual metaphors.

It is important to avoid simpleminded dichotomies when talking about metaphor. Metaphors have many statuses. One cannot just talk of them as being basic versus nonbasic, poetic versus everyday, conventionalized versus nonconventionalized, and so on. Metaphors differ along many parameters, and often the difference is a matter of degree. There are certain parameters that we have given a lot of weight to in this discussion. One of them is binary: conceptual versus linguistic. We have to distinguish metaphorical thought from the language that expresses that thought.

A second major parameter is conventionalization. This applies at both the conceptual and linguistic levels. At the conceptual level, a metaphor is conventional to the extent that it is automatic, effortless, and generally established as a mode of thought among members of a linguistic community. For example, DEATH IS DEPARTURE is deeply conventionalized at the conceptual level; we probably all have it. Though a basic metaphor like LIFE IS BONDAGE might be deeply conventionalized for a particular subcommunity (such as certain Christian communities), nonetheless it is not as conventionalized across the whole community of speakers of English as is DEATH IS DEPARTURE.

Conventionalization also applies to the *connection* between the conceptual and linguistic levels. When, in this book, we speak of the degree to which a conceptual metaphor is conventionalized in the language, we mean the extent to which it underlies a range of everyday linguistic expressions. For example, DEATH IS DEPARTURE is not just conventionalized as a way of conceiving of death; it is also widely conventionalized in language, underlying a wide range of expressions such as "pass away," be "no longer with us," "gone," "among the dear departed," and so on.

A third major parameter along which metaphors may differ is what we have loosely called basicness. The basicness of a metaphor is its conceptual indispensability. Take, for example, PURPOSES ARE DESTINATIONS and TIME MOVES. It is virtually unthinkable for any speaker of English (as well as many other languages) to dispense with these metaphors for conceptualizing purposes and time. To do so would be to change utterly the way we think about goals and the future. That is what we mean by saying that such metaphors are basic to the conceptual system on which our language and our culture are based. On the other end of the scale, the metaphor that the evening is a patient etherized upon a table is quite dispensable for the ways we think and for the structure of our conceptual system. And our lives do not noticeably differ if we do not happen to have this metaphor. Somewhere in the middle of the gradient is a basic conceptual metaphor like LIFE IS A FIRE. We probably all have this basic conceptual metaphor, and we use it to some extent in our thinking. But, in the main, relatively little would change in our thinking or our lives if we did not have this conceptual metaphor. It is more dispensable than LIFE IS A JOURNEY, and less dispensable than Eliot's metaphor of the evening as a patient etherized upon a table.

In short, a serious study of metaphor must address a wide and complex set of theoretical issues. Let us turn to them now.

TWO

The Power of Poetic Metaphor

What Is Not Metaphorical

To understand what is metaphorical, we must begin with what is not metaphorical. In brief, to the extent that a concept is understood and structured on its own terms—without making use of structure imported from a completely different conceptual domain—we will say that it is not metaphorical.

The word "extent" was chosen with care. A given concept may be metaphorically understood and structured in some respects but not in others. Consider dogs, for example. We do not conventionally understand a dog's appearance via a mapping between it and a completely different conceptual domain. Thus, part of our conceptualization of a dog is nonmetaphorical: the four legs, wagging tail, cold wet black nose, and so on. Of course, we may invent all the metaphors we please in which nonmetaphorical concepts are targets. We might say, for instance, that a dog's wagging tail is its flag, signaling to us. But this does not mean that the wagging tail cannot be understood nonmetaphorically as just a tail; to the extent that it is so understood it is not metaphorical. Moreover, the dog's tail is not conventionally, automatically, and unconsciously understood as a flag. That is, the tail-as-flag metaphor is not part of our *conventional* concept of a dog's tail. So far as we can tell, there is nothing metaphorical about the conventional concept of a dog's tail.

But when we understand a dog as being "loyal," we are understanding an instinctive property of the dog in terms of a human personality trait. When we conceptualize a dog as "loyal," we are conceptualizing that aspect of the dog via metaphor. In short, it is misleading to think of concepts as a whole as being either all metaphorical or all nonmetaphorical. Metaphoricity has to do with particular aspects of conceptual structure. Part of a concept's structure can be understood metaphorically, using structure imported from another domain, while part may be understood directly, that is, without metaphor.

As we have seen, death is understood via a range of metaphors. But, of course, death is in part understood directly as well: when one is alive, one is functioning; when one is dead, one is not functioning. This is a nonmetaphorical aspect of our understanding of death. As such, it can be used as the source domain for other metaphors. For example, if we say "The phone is dead," we are using the general MACHINES ARE PEOPLE metaphor, which maps human death onto the failure of the machine to operate. It is the *nonmetaphorical* understanding of death that is mapped in this metaphor—not the metaphorical understanding of death in terms of departure, cold, darkness, and so on. The metaphorical understanding of death is used to comprehend other aspects of death than mere nonfunctionality.

Light is another example of a concept that is partially understood on its own terms and partially understood via metaphor. We perceive light, react to it emotionally, and know that it allows us to see things. But light as a scientific phenomenon requires a further understanding. We have two common scientific metaphors for light: as waves and as particles that move faster than anything else in the universe. But this metaphorical understanding of light is not used in the metaphor by which we understand life as light. The aspects of the concept of light we use in the life-as-light metaphor have nothing to do with the metaphorical conception of light either as particles or as waves. The life-as-light metaphor depends instead on certain nonmetaphorical knowledge about light: that it promotes growth, that it makes us happy for the most part, that it allows us to see and gain the knowledge necessary for our survival, and so on. Thus light has an aspect independent of the particle and wave metaphors, an aspect which is used as the basis for the metaphorical understanding of other concepts. It also has an aspect (namely, its physical nature) which is metaphorically understood and is not used as the basis for other metaphors.

The idea that metaphoricity is all or none arises from the fact that we have a range of concepts that are not normally understood metaphorically at all. Things that we think of as being straightforwardly physical—rocks and trees and arms and legs—are usually things that we have conceptualized not metaphorically but rather in terms of what we take to be our bodily experience. In addition, the source domains of many metaphors are typically understood without metaphor. Thus, departures, journeys, plants, fire, sleep, days and nights, heat and cold, possessions, burdens, and locations are not themselves metaphorically understood, at least insofar as they form a basis for the metaphorical understanding of other concepts. We conventionally understand these concepts not by virtue of metaphoric mappings between them and different conceptual domains but rather by virtue of their grounding in what we take to be our forms of life, our habitual and routine bodily and social experiences.

Of course, just because these conceptualizations are nonmetaphoric does not mean that they are mind-free. It does not mean that they are somehow given to us directly by the objective world. On the contrary, cultural anthropologists often investigate just the ways that experience is understood differently in different cultures. But their grounding is not metaphoric. It is instead in patterns of what we take to be habitual and routine experience, both biological and social, that we know unconsciously and in rich interactional detail, because we live these patterns.

In the case of profoundly conventionalized conceptual metaphors, such as the basic metaphors we discuss in this book, aspects of one concept, the target, are understood in terms of nonmetaphoric aspects of another concept, the source. A metaphor with the name A IS B is a mapping of part of the structure of our knowledge of source domain B onto target domain A. Before we can discuss the nature of such mappings, we must first discuss what the structure of knowledge in a conceptual domain is like.

Metaphor and Knowledge

Understanding any poem requires knowledge. We take for granted much of the everyday knowledge we need to understand poetry. Take, for example, the following poem from the Sanskrit tradition.

> Neighbor please
> keep an eye on my house
> my husband says the water from the well
> is tasteless
> so even when I'm alone
> I have to go into the forest
> where the Tamāla trees
> shade the river-bank
> and maybe the thick reeds
> will leave marks on my body[1]

The poem presupposes the common knowledge that passionate sexual activity can leave marks on the body. It also takes for granted the knowledge that, in India at the time of the poem, illicit sexual liaisons commonly took place in the tall, thick reeds along river banks. Without such knowledge about reeds, we would not be able to make sense of another Sanskrit poem:

> There where the reeds are tall
> is the best place to cross the river
> she told the traveller
> with her eye on him
> (*The Peacock's Egg*, p. 155)

Conventional metaphor, of course, also depends on conventional knowledge. In order to understand a target domain in terms of a source domain, one must have appropriate knowledge of the source domain. Take, for example, the LIFE IS A JOURNEY metaphor that we discussed in chapter one. Our understanding of life as a journey uses our knowledge about journeys. All journeys involve travelers, paths

---

[1] W. S. Merwin and J. Moussaieff Masson, trans., *Sanskrit Love Poetry* (New York: Columbia University Press, 1977). Copyright © 1977 Columbia University Press. Used by permission. Reprinted as *The Peacock's Egg* (San Francisco: North Point Press, 1981), p. 101.

traveled, places where we start, and places where we have been. Some journeys are purposeful and have destinations that we set out for, while others may involve wandering without any destination in mind. To understand life as a journey is to have in mind, consciously or more likely unconsciously, a correspondence between a traveler and a person living the life, the road traveled and the "course" of a lifetime, a starting point and the time of birth, and so on.

One of the reasons that this form of understanding is powerful is that it makes use of a general knowledge of journeys. This knowledge has a skeletal structure rich enough to distinguish journeys from other kinds of activities, but not so rich as to rule out any particular kind of journey. As a consequence, the understanding of life as a journey permits not just a single simpleminded conceptualization of life but rather a rich and varied one. Because our knowledge of journeys includes options for types of journeys, the metaphorical understanding of life in terms of a journey includes options for a corresponding variety of understandings of life. To the extent that one views life as purposeful, those purposes are viewed as destinations, and we can act accordingly by setting out to reach them, getting around impediments, and accepting guidance. Correspondingly, to the extent that we see life as not involving purposes, we can view our journey as wandering and observing the landscape.

Two things permit such richness: the structure of our knowledge of journeys and our ability to map from that structured knowledge to a conception of life. The structure of our knowledge of journeys can be seen as having well-differentiated components such as travelers, a starting point, a path, impediments, and so on; some are required and some, like destinations, vehicles, companions, and guides, are optional. We will call knowledge structured in such a skeletal form a "schema," and we will use the term "slots" for elements of a schema that are to be filled in. Thus, a JOURNEY schema has a slot for TRAVELER that can be filled by any particular person whom we understand to be on a journey. Indeed, the very concept of a traveler can be defined only relative to the concept of a journey. Understanding that someone is a traveler is understanding that he fills the role of TRAVELER in a JOURNEY schema.

The metaphor LIFE IS A JOURNEY is thus a mapping of the structure of the JOURNEY schema onto the domain of LIFE in such a way as to set up the appropriate correspondences between TRAVELER and PERSON LEADING A LIFE, between STARTING POINT and BIRTH, and so on.

Part of the power of such a metaphor is its ability to *create* structure in our understanding of life. Life, after all, *need* not be viewed as a journey. It *need* not be viewed as having a path, or destinations, or impediments to travel, or vehicles. That structuring of our understanding of life comes from the structure of our knowledge about journeys. When we reason about life in terms of destinations, forks in the road, roadblocks, guides, and so on, we are importing patterns of inference from the domain of journeys to the domain of life. For example, we can infer from the fact that someone is spinning his wheels that he is not getting anywhere and will not reach his destination. We can infer from the fact that someone has hit a roadblock that if he is to continue on he must deal with it in some way: remove it, get over it, get around it, or find another route. Much of our reasoning about life involves inferences of this sort. Thus, the power to reason about so abstract an idea as life comes very largely through metaphor.

We understand and reason using our conceptual system, which includes an inventory of structures, of which schemas and metaphors are established parts. Once we learn a schema, we do not have to learn it again or make it up fresh each time we use it. It becomes conventionalized and as such is used automatically, effortlessly, and even unconsciously. That is part of the power of schemas: we can use these ready tools without having to put any energy into making or finding them. Similarly, once we learn a conceptual metaphor, it too is just there, conventionalized, a ready and powerful conceptual tool—automatic, effortless, and largely unconscious. The things most alive in our conceptual system are those things that we use constantly, unconsciously, and automatically. They include conceptual schemas and conceptual metaphors.

For the same reasons that schemas and metaphors give us power to conceptualize and reason, so they have power over us. Anything that we rely on constantly, unconsciously, and automatically is so much part of us that it cannot be easily resisted, in large measure because it is barely even noticed. To the extent that we use a conceptual schema or a conceptual metaphor, we accept its validity. Consequently, when someone else uses it, we are predisposed to accept its validity. For this reason, conventionalized schemas and metaphors have *persuasive* power over us.

At this point we can see how that power arises. Metaphors have an internal structure. Each metaphorical mapping consists of the following:

— Slots in the source-domain schema (e.g., journey), which get mapped onto slots in the target domain (e.g., life). In some cases the target-domain slots exist independently of the metaphoric mapping. For example, the traveler slot gets mapped onto the living person slot, which exists in the domain of life independently of the metaphoric mapping. Other target domain slots are *created* by the mapping. For example, to map the PATH slot of the JOURNEY schema into the domain of life means understanding the events of one's life as constituting the points of a path, which necessitates creating a COURSE OF LIFE slot in the LIFE domain.

— Relations in the source domain (journey), which get mapped onto relations in the target domain (life). For example, take the idea of a traveler reaching a destination he set out for. This maps onto the idea of a person achieving a purpose in life. So the source domain relation REACHING holding between TRAVELER and DESTINATION gets mapped onto the target domain relation ACHIEVING holding between PERSON and PURPOSE.

— Properties in the source domain, which get mapped onto properties in the target domain. For example, a traveler has strengths and weaknesses which affect the way he conducts the journey, deals with impediments, and so on. This maps onto the idea of a person having strengths and weaknesses for conducting life, for dealing with problems, and so on. Thus if we can say of someone that

63

he is strong enough to roll over anything that gets in his way, we are saying with this metaphor something about his way of dealing with difficulties in his life.

— Knowledge in the source domain, which gets mapped onto knowledge in the target domain. Our knowledge of a domain allows us to draw inferences about that domain. When a domain serves as a source domain for a metaphoric mapping, inference patterns in the source domain are mapped onto the target domain. For example, if you hit a dead end, you cannot go on in the same direction and have to find another route. If you hit a metaphorical dead end in life, you must find another course of action.

We have now identified the following sources of the power of metaphor:

— *The power to structure.* Metaphorical mappings allow us to impart to a concept structure which is not there independent of the metaphor. Death—one's own and that of others—is an important part of human life that we seek ways to comprehend. If death is conceived of as a departure, then it becomes natural to conceive of death as the beginning of another journey, like the journey of life, with a final destination of its own. Only if we conceive of death in this way can we ponder the nature of the final destination.

— *The power of options.* Schemas are very general, as they must be to cover the range of possible instantiations. Options about what details will fill out a schema occur at higher and lower levels. At the most general level, there are optional components in a schema: a journey may or may not have a vehicle, a guide, a companion, provisions, and so on. The fact that the components of a schema are slots that can be filled in by more specific information provides for options at lower levels. For example, a journey may be either on land or on sea or through the air or through space. The JOURNEY schema contains the concept VEHICLE as an option, but not the concept CAR, which is a more specific kind of vehicle. An expression like "the fast lane" fills in the VEHICLE slot with the special case, CAR. The phrase "life in the fast lane" thus uses the LIFE IS A JOURNEY metaphor, with the VEHICLE slot in the JOURNEY schema filled in by CAR and the PATH slot filled in by THE FAST LANE. Such options allow us to enrich the basic metaphorical structure and derive new understandings of the target domain.

— *The power of reason.* Metaphors allow us to borrow patterns of inference from the source domain to use in reasoning about some target domain. For example, the LIFE IS A JOURNEY metaphor is one of the most powerful tools we have for making sense of our lives and for making decisions about what to do and even what to believe. If, on a journey, we come to a dead end, then we must find another route to continue making progress. Similarly, if we think of our situation in life as a dead end, then we can reason accordingly: we can stay put and make no progress, or we can find another way to achieve our purposes.

— *The power of evaluation.* We not only import entities and structure from the source domain to the target domain, we also carry over the way we evaluate the entities in the source domain. For example, when we speak of life as a "dead end" we are viewing an unchanging state in a negative light as a lack of progress, rather than, for instance, viewing life in terms of the security and stability that could result from stasis.

— *The power of being there.* The very existence and availability of conventional conceptual metaphors makes them powerful as conceptual and expressive tools. But they have power over us for the same reason. Because they can be used so automatically and effortlessly, we find it hard to question them, if we can even notice them.

Cognitive Models and Commonplace Knowledge

Conceptual schemas organize our knowledge. They constitute cognitive models of some aspect of the world, models that we use in comprehending our experience and in reasoning about it. Cognitive models are not conscious models; they are unconscious and used automatically and effortlessly. We cannot observe them directly; they are inferred from their effects. Of course, we can consciously consider and try to get at what our unconscious models might be, as we have done throughout this book in the case of metaphorical mappings.

We acquire cognitive models in at least two ways: by our own direct experience and through our culture. Thus, people who have never seen millstones can nonetheless learn, via their culture, that they are used in mills to grind grain, and that they are the enormous round flat stones that rotate about an axis. Cognitive models that are acquired via our culture are typically models that are long-standing in the culture. Cultural models of this sort are often at variance with our scientific knowledge. For example, experts on wolves maintain that wolves avoid humans whenever they can; nevertheless, our cultural model of wolves sees them as vicious beasts that attack humans without provocation, often cruelly.

Some cognitive models are very abstract. For example, we comprehend people, animals, and objects in the world as having attributes, some of which are essential to their nature. Things in the world may or may not actually have essential attributes, but we understand them as having them. This is part of a very general cognitive model that we have of the nature of things and how they behave. We also commonly ascribe the behavior of people, animals and objects to some attribute that they have, as when we think of someone who *typically acts* angrily as *being* an angry person. In such a case, we conceive of his behavior as a consequence of an attribute of his.

In chapter four, we will introduce a large-scale cognitive model—the Great Chain of Being—which ranges over the full gamut of forms of being in the universe. It is a cognitive model that we use to make sense of, and impose order on, the universe. It is acquired culturally, at least in its extended forms, and in describing it we are, of course, not suggesting that the universe really conforms to the model.

We will refer to such cognitive models in various ways throughout this book, depending on what aspect of them we wish to stress. We have called them "cognitive models" here to stress their mental nature and to distinguish them from any claim that they represent scientific reality. We will call them "cultural models" when it seems most appropriate to stress their cultural nature, "commonplace models" when the their everyday character is at issue, and "commonplace notions" when the term "model" seems too grandiose for such a simple idea.

The Conceptual Power of Poetic Metaphor

Poetic thought uses the mechanisms of everyday thought, but it extends them, elaborates them, and combines them in ways that go beyond the ordinary.

EXTENDING

One major mode of poetic thought is to take a convention-alized metaphor and extend it. Consider, for example, the conventional metaphor DEATH IS SLEEP. That conventional metaphor is, of course, partial—it does not map everything in our general knowledge of sleep onto death but only certain aspects: inactivity, inability to perceive, horizontal position, and so on. In Hamlet's soliloquy, Shakespeare extends the ordinary conventional metaphor of death as sleep to include the possibility of dreaming:

> To sleep? Perchance to dream! Ay, there's the rub;
> For in that sleep of death what dreams may come?

ELABORATING

Another principal mode of poetic thought that goes beyond the ordinary is the nonconventional elaborating of schemas, by filling in slots in unusual ways rather than by extending the metaphor to map additional slots. As always, when we say that the poet is elaborating the schema or extending the metaphor, we mean that we, the readers, are doing the elaborating and extending in ways that we take to be indicated or at least suggested by the poem. For example, let us consider a passage that can be elaborated in more than one way: Horace's reference to death as the "eternal exile of the raft."

According to the conventional metaphor of death as departure, we conceive of death as departure away from here, without possibility of return, on a journey, perhaps in a vehicle. The conventionalized metaphor is no more specific than that. We may take it that Horace is using this metaphor but filling in the slots, that is, elaborating it, in an interesting way. Being away from here is characterized by the special case of exile. The vehicle is an unusual one—a raft. These ways of making the DEATH IS DEPARTURE metaphor specific add considerable conceptual content to the metaphor of death as departure. Exile, after all, is not merely being away from here. It is banishment; it is unwanted; it assumes that one would prefer to return; it is an unnatural state; and so on. A raft, moreover, is not something that takes us swiftly, directly, luxuriously, or securely to a given destination. It is something we are not in control of because we are at the whim of the currents, and it leaves us exposed to the elements. We can take Horace to mean by "eternal exile" that we are forever out on the raft. In that case, the raft does not even have a destination. This elaborating of the death-as-departure metaphor in such an unconventional way results in our understanding death differently and reasoning about it differently. Compare Horace's use of death as departure with Dickinson's special case of the same general conventional metaphor:

> Afraid? Of whom am I afraid?
> Not Death, for who is He?
> The porter of my father's lodge
> As much abasheth me.

Dickinson includes the destination, and fills in the destination as home ("my father's lodge"). The way we have read the Horace poem denies the existence of any destination at all. For Dickinson death is not fearful, whereas for Horace it is. Thus, filling in the same conventional metaphor in different ways can lead us to different conclusions about how we should feel about death.

Of course, there is another reading of Horace's phrase, a more conventional one. One can read Horace as merely referring by the "eternal exile of the raft" to the raft of

Charon, who takes dead souls across the Styx to their eternal exile in the underworld. If we read the phrase that way, then Horace's filling in of the death-as-departure metaphor still remains very different from Dickinson's: in both there is a destination, but in Dickinson's poem it is home, and in Horace's poem it is exile, the opposite of home.

QUESTIONING

In addition to elaborating conventional metaphor, poets go beyond the normal use of conventional metaphor to point out, and call into question, the boundaries of our everyday metaphorical understandings of important concepts. Indeed, the major poetic point being made can be the inadequacy of the conventional metaphor. As Catullus says,

> Suns can set and return again,
> but when our brief light goes out,
> there's one perpetual night to be slept through.
> (Catullus 5)

Here Catullus is both using A LIFETIME IS A DAY and pointing out the breakdown of that metaphor at the crucial point, namely, mortality.

A similar case occurs in the passage from *Othello* cited in chapter one, where Othello contemplates killing Desdemona and says to a lighted candle,

> If I quench thee, thou flaming minister,
> I can again thy former light restore,
> Should I repent me; but once put out thy light,
> Thou cunning'st pattern of excelling nature,
> I know not where is that Promethean heat
> That can thy light relume.

Still another case occurs in the Sanskrit tradition, where the concept of release is central and is typically understood metaphorically as the absence of emotions and qualities. Here the poet challenges the metaphor, suggesting that a sensual letting go is better than nothingness as a metaphor for release:

> Some in this world insist
> that a certain whatever-it-is

that has no taste of
joy or sorrow
no qualities
is Release
they are fools
to my mind the
body unfurling
with joy of being young
flowering out of love
her eyes floating as with wine and
words wandering with love
then the undoing of the knot
of her sari
that
is Release
(*The Peacock's Egg*, p. 167)

COMPOSING

Finally, let us turn to what is perhaps the most powerful of all ways in which poetic thought goes beyond the ordinary way we use conventional metaphoric thought: the formation of composite metaphors. As we have seen, there may be more than one conventional metaphor for a given target domain. For example, life may be viewed metaphorically both as a day and as a precious possession. One of the things that characterizes poetic thought is the simultaneous use of two or more such metaphors in the same passage, or even in the same sentence. Take a quatrain from the Shakespeare sonnet we discussed in chapter one:

> In me thou seest the twilight of such day
> As after sunset fadeth in the west;
> Which by and by black night doth take away,
> Death's second self that seals up all in rest.

As we saw before, there are at least five conventional conceptual metaphors sculpted into the composite metaphorical conception of death we find in this quatrain. They are LIGHT IS A SUBSTANCE, EVENTS ARE ACTIONS, LIFE IS A PRECIOUS POSSESSION, A LIFETIME IS A DAY, and LIFE IS LIGHT.

Consider the simple clause "black night doth take away

[the twilight]" as it appears in the passage above. We understand this clause to contain a composite of the metaphors that a lifetime is a day and death is night, that light is a substance, that a life is a precious possession, and that events are actions. The metaphors are composed in such a way that night is identified as the agent who takes away the light, which is understood metaphorically as life, and consequently seen as stealing a precious possession. In this line, virtually as many conceptual metaphors as words are used. The formation of the metaphorical composite takes place at the conceptual level, and is very complex. For example, in this case, LIGHT IS A SUBSTANCE produces a conception of light which is the kind of thing that could be taken away. A LIFETIME IS A DAY identifies life as light, which in turn identifies it as a substance. LIFE IS A PRECIOUS POSSESSION identifies life as something we don't want taken away. And EVENTS ARE ACTIONS allows the event of death to be seen as caused by an agent, who in turn is identified as the person who takes away the precious possession. The point is that the work here is conceptual, a matter of putting complex metaphorical concepts together rather than merely putting words together.

The mode of metaphorical thought that poets use and invoke in their readers goes beyond ordinary metaphoric thought by including these elements:

— The novel extension of the metaphor to include elements otherwise not mapped, such as extending DEATH IS SLEEP to dreaming.

— The imaginative filling in of special cases, such as having the vehicle in DEATH IS DEPARTURE be a coach.

— The formation of composite metaphors in which two or more conventional metaphors are joined together in ways that they ordinarily would not be. Its effect is to produce a richer and more complex set of metaphorical connections, which gives inferences beyond those that follow from each of the metaphors alone.

— Explicit commentary on the limitations of conceptual metaphors, and the offering of an alternative.

These extensions are a large part of what makes poetic metaphor more interesting than conventional metaphor.

They allow the use of ordinary conceptual resources in extraordinary ways. It is by these means that poets lead us beyond the bounds of ordinary modes of thought and guide us beyond the automatic and unconscious everyday use of metaphor. What makes poetic metaphor noticeable and memorable is thus the special, nonautomatic use to which ordinary, automatic modes of thought are put.

Personification

Poetic composition is like musical composition. Just as the composer combines the simple elements of tonality—notes and chords and harmonies—into musical phrases and musical movements of great richness and complexity, so the poet combines ordinary concepts, everyday metaphors, and the most mundane knowledge to form conceptual compositions, orchestrations of ideas that we perceive as rich and complex wholes. Complex metaphors are such compositions. Their power derives from the power of the conventional elements of which they are composed as well as from the power that comes from putting those elements together to transcend the simple components.

The power of poetic composition to create complex new ideas from simpler conventional ideas reveals itself in especially clear form in personification—metaphors through which we understand other things as people. As human beings, we can best understand other things in our own terms. Personification permits us to use our knowledge about ourselves to maximal effect, to use insights about ourselves to help us comprehend such things as forces of nature, common events, abstract concepts, and inanimate objects. For example, consider Yehuda Amichai's

> The world is awake tonight.
> It is lying on its back, with its eyes open.[2]

Here, the absence of overt events is understood in terms of the inactivity of a person, via EVENTS ARE ACTIONS. Since a person lying on his back at night with his eyes open would

[2] Yehuda Amichai, *Selected Poetry*, ed. and trans. Chana Block and Stephen Mitchell (New York: Harper and Row, 1986), p. 4

72

be attentive, so the world is seen as attentive, noticing things it would not normally notice, instead of being a sleeping and therefore indifferent world.

In another passage, Amichai personifies "the coming day":

> I'll wake up early and bribe the coming day
> to be kind to us.
> (*Selected Poetry*, p. 4)

External events affect us in ways we cannot control, and via EVENTS ARE ACTIONS we can understand those events as actions by a world we cannot control. Through the metonymy of the time period ("the coming day") standing for the state of the world during that period, the coming day is seen as the actor who performs those events. In the logic of this metaphor, maybe one can deal with that actor the way one deals with others who are in control, namely by bribing him. The word "bribe" invokes both the EVENTS ARE ACTIONS metaphor and the accompanying personification metaphor, since the individual bribed is normally required to be human.

Not all metaphors that map from persons in the source domain are personifications. In some metaphors, a person in one schema is understood in terms of a person in another. For example, LIFE IS A JOURNEY maps a traveler who is a person in the source domain onto a person in the target domain. In other metaphors, we understand a person in terms of something that is not a person; for example, PEOPLE ARE PLANTS maps a plant in the source domain onto a person in the target domain. But understanding death as a footman is a personification because though death is not inherently a person, it is being understood as a person through the metaphor of death-as-departure, in which the footman escorts you.

Conceiving of death as a footman is simple, immediate, and natural, like the great variety of personifications that we saw in chapter one: death as a reaper, time as a devourer, and so on. What makes these immediate and natural is that they arise as a consequence of composition from other more basic conceptual resources.

In chapter one we observed, in loose terms, that death

can be personified as a reaper because we have a basic meta-phor that people are plants; that time can be a changer because of our commonsense notion that the passage of time plays a causal role in bringing about events, especially changes; that time can be a thief because we have the fur-ther metaphor that life is a precious possession, and so on. But we also observed that the personification of death as a reaper does not come solely from understanding people as plants with respect to their life cycle, since the life cycle of plants in nature does not include a reaper. The reaper only enters in the special scenario of planting, cultivation, and harvesting. Similarly, the personification of time as a thief does not come solely from the general metaphor that life is a precious possession, since the most general case of that metaphor has no thieves, but only the loss of life. Again, the thief enters only in the special scenario.

What we saw in chapter one was that all such personifi-cations we discussed there arose in roughly the same way: from a composition of the metaphor EVENTS ARE ACTIONS (which introduced an agent) with some further knowledge that characterized the nature of the event and the nature of that agent. Sometimes this further knowledge came from a basic metaphor like PEOPLE ARE PLANTS, sometimes from the cultural model that THE PASSAGE OF TIME PLAYS A CAUSAL ROLE IN EVENTS OF CHANGE, and sometimes from both, as when this cultural model combines with the meta-phor LIFE IS A PRECIOUS POSSESSION to give us the means to understand time as a thief.

To say that such instances of personification arise through composition is to say something remarkable:

> We can produce an indefinitely large number of in-stances of personification from metaphors that do not themselves contain any personifications. All we need to do is to put those metaphors and bits of nonmeta-phorical knowledge together in the right way.

How is it possible to get personifications from metaphors that are not personifications? How can we manipulate our conceptual resources in such a way that we can create ways of understanding other things in terms of ourselves? The answer comes from the basic mechanisms of combination that we discussed in the previous section: forming combinations of existing metaphors and filling in their slots in interesting ways. At the center of the process of composition resulting in personification is the EVENTS ARE ACTIONS metaphor.

This metaphor differs in two respects from the others we have discussed so far. First, the source domain of actions is a subcategory of the target category of events; that is, every action is an event, though the converse is not true. Indeed, it is exactly the events without agents that the EVENTS ARE ACTIONS metaphor applies to. For example, natural death can be seen as being a death at the hand of an agent. Or the natural loss of youthful powers can be seen as caused by some agency, as in "time, the subtle thief of youth."

Second, because actions are events, the mapping from actions to events has a structure somewhat different from other mappings. Each action consists of an event plus the agency which brings that event about. The mapping thus adds structure to the event domain, making the event the result of an action and introducing the agent who brings that action about.

To see how this works in detail, let us consider how we arrive at an understanding of death as a reaper. First, the EVENTS ARE ACTIONS metaphor structures the event of death as the result of an action and adds to the event of death an agent who brings that event about. Second, the PEOPLE ARE PLANTS metaphor can be elaborated via a scenario of cultivation of plants, in which the plants at the end of their life cycle are harvested. The source domain of harvesting may contain a reaper, which, as we saw above, is not inherently part of the mapping from plants onto people. Third, the action of harvesting is identified as the relevant action in the EVENTS ARE ACTIONS metaphor, and the agent of death is identified as the reaper, who is the agent of harvesting in the harvest scenario. It is by this mechanism that the reaper, who is not conventionally mapped by the PEOPLE ARE PLANTS metaphor, gets to be mapped as a result of the composition of PEOPLE ARE PLANTS with EVENTS ARE ACTIONS.

Personifications can result from the interaction of the EVENTS ARE ACTIONS metaphor with cultural models or commonplace knowledge, as well as with other metaphors. Take, for example, the cultural model that THE PASSAGE OF TIME PLAYS A CAUSAL ROLE IN EVENTS OF CHANGE. The schema for an action contains a causal relationship between an event and something else—the agent who is responsible for the event. Suppose the event is a change of some kind. By composing the metaphor with the cultural model in which the passage of time is a cause of change, we can view time metaphorically as an agent who causes change. The result of this process of composition is the TIME IS A CHANGER metaphor, in which time appears personified because it has been identified as the agent in the metaphor EVENTS ARE ACTIONS.

Because TIME IS A CHANGER is so general as to cover all events of change, it invites further specification through further composition. One kind of change is a change of value. The agent of such a change is an evaluator. By specifying the change as a change of value, we make Time the changer into Time the evaluator.

Time itself involves change, since the present changes into the immediate future. By the TIME IS SOMETHING MOVING metaphor, we understand change of time as change of location. By the EVENTS ARE ACTIONS metaphor we can understand an event of change of location as resulting from an action by an agent. If the agent is identical to the thing moving, we get a case of self-propulsion: time can be running, creeping, trotting, and so on. As Shakespeare says in *As You Like It,* act three, scene two:

> Time travels in divers paces with divers persons. I'll tell
> you who Time ambles withal, who Time trots withal,
> who Time gallops withal. . . .

In each of the cases above, personifications are produced from metaphors which are not personifications by a composition of a metaphor with either another metaphor, some commonplace knowledge, or both. But such compositions do not merely produce personifications of some kind or other; rather, what we know about the event in the target domain restricts the possibilities for personification. For example, if we conceive of death as going completely out of existence forever, and if we furthermore understand that event as an action, then the action we choose must make something go completely out of existence forever. The actions of a devourer suit this constraint, and thus it is possible to see death as a devourer. Contrast this with a personification that will not work: a magician who makes things disappear for a few moments and then reappear. Eternal death cannot be personified by such a magician. Of course, if we conceive of death as being transformed from one thing into another via reincarnation, a magician who can turn something into something else might be a suitable personification.

This constraint is a natural consequence of the EVENTS ARE ACTIONS metaphor. If an event is to be understood in terms of an action, then the general shape of the action must conform to the general shape of the event. For example, if the event is instantaneous, then so must the action be instantaneous. If the event is repetitive, then the action must be repetitive. If the event preserves objects, then the action must preserve objects. In our standard conception, death does not preserve objects; once they go out of existence, they do not return. But the magician example just cited does preserve objects; the objects that disappear then reappear. The general shape of the magician's action thus does not conform to the general shape of the event of death as we normally understand it. The EVENTS ARE ACTIONS metaphor does not provide specific details of the personification, but it does constrain them. The nature of the mapping explains why certain personifications are appropriate and others are not.

Consider a further example. Part of the general shape of an event is the chain of causality that structures the event. In an action, there is a causal relationship between what the agent does and the result of the action. Events without agents may also have a causal structure. For example, time is seen as playing a causal role in natural healing, because healing occurs with the passage of time. Because the EVENTS ARE ACTIONS metaphor preserves the general shape of events, it also preserves *causal* shape: the causal chain from agent to event in the source domain of action must be mapped onto a causal chain from something else to the event in the target domain of events. Therefore, because there is a causal link between time and natural healing, we can personify time as the agent who brings about the healing in sentences like "Time heals all wounds." Similarly, if we know that vitamin E plays a causal role in healing, then we can personify vitamin E as a healer. But because there is no causal link between, say, pain or hospital bills and healing, we cannot view them as agents of healing, and therefore it would be strange to personify pain or our hospital bills as a healer. Not every concomitant of an event can be assigned a causal role.

There is another class of cases in which EVENTS ARE ACTIONS preserves a causal chain and thus permits a personification. Take examples like "Death cut him down" or "Death took him from us" or "Death is a reaper." In such cases, we are making use of our knowledge of death: each of us dies because death, as a general phenomenon, is inevitable. The general phenomenon of death is thus seen as playing a causal role in each of our particular deaths. When we compose EVENTS ARE ACTIONS with this commonplace notion, death (the general phenomenon) can be understood as an agent who brings about individual events of death. Thus, relative to this commonplace notion, causal shape is preserved by EVENTS ARE ACTIONS: the causal link between the agent and the event in the action domain (e.g., reaping) corresponds to the causal link between the single general cause, death, and the individual event of death it causes. "Death" in sentences like "Death is a reaper" refers to death-in-general: that is why it is the same reaper who claims all of our lives.

The EVENTS ARE ACTIONS metaphor thus has extraordinary explanatory power. Not only does it allow us to account for all of the personifications that we found in chapter one, but its character of preserving the general shape of events allows us to explain why certain things can serve as personifications while others cannot. At this point, there is only one further general constraint on personifications that remains to be explained: the appearance and character of the personification. For example, why is the reaper grim? And why must Time the healer be portrayed as looking very different from Time the devourer?

The way we feel about the appearance and character of the personification must correspond to the way we feel about the event. For example, if we feel that the event of healing is benign and comforting, then Time the healer cannot appear terrifying and malicious to us. Time the devourer may be portrayed as a monster, but Time the healer had better not be. This is not a separate constraint but a consequence of the way we reason about the source and target domains with respect to each other. The EVENTS ARE ACTIONS metaphor links the EVENT in the EVENT domain to the corresponding EVENT in the ACTION domain, and consequently to the action that caused that event. Thus, our feelings about the event must correspond to our feelings about the action.

There is also a common tendency for people to project their feelings about events onto the actors who cause them. If we get angry at the breaking of a window, we typically get angry at the person who broke it. Correspondingly, since healing is benign, in "Time is healer" we see the agent of healing, time, as benign. Thus, constraints on the appearance and character of a personified agent follow from the nature of the personification process.

A more complicated example of the same constraint arises with personifications like DEATH IS A REAPER, which arises from a composition of EVENTS ARE ACTIONS with PEOPLE ARE PLANTS. As we observed in chapter one, there is a reason why the reaper must be grim: our feelings about the reaper must conform to our feelings about death. This should be an instance of the same constraint, that our attitude about the event is projected onto our attitude about the agent who caused the event. But here the addition of the PEOPLE ARE PLANTS metaphor makes things slightly more complex. In the case cited above, our feelings about the healer conformed to our feelings about healing; healing and the healer are in the same conceptual domain. But here, our feelings about the reaper conform to our feelings about death, and

death and the reaper are in different conceptual domains—
LIFE and PLANTS—and are related only by the metaphor.
The PEOPLE ARE PLANTS metaphor is thus the crucial link
in the explanation: our feelings of death are projected onto
the agent of death, which via the metaphor is identified as
the reaper.

The process of personification illustrates what is perhaps
the most impressive of the powers of metaphorical thought:
the power to create, with naturalness and ease. In all the
cases we have discussed, personifications are created by composition, and the process of creation uses only the common-
est of materials and operations: the EVENTS ARE ACTIONS
metaphor, commonplace knowledge, cognitive models, other
conventional metaphors, and the process of composition.
The materials are so ready to hand that we hardly notice
they are there, and the process of composition is so automatic, so natural and so common, that it takes an act of
analysis to tease apart the composite elements. Yet they allow for an explanation of all of the basic properties of such
personifications, including their very existence.

Generic-level metaphors

We have used the term "basic metaphor" to refer to any
conceptual metaphor whose use is conventional, unconscious, automatic, and typically unnoticed. So far we have
talked about basic metaphors as if they were all of one type.
But, as we just saw in our discussion of personification, the
EVENTS ARE ACTIONS metaphor is unlike other metaphors.
In a metaphor like LIFE IS A JOURNEY, there is a designated
ontological mapping: a certain list of slots in the JOURNEY
schema maps in exactly one way onto a corresponding list
of slots in the LIFE schema (e.g., DESTINATIONS correspond
to LIFE GOALS). But in the EVENTS ARE ACTIONS metaphor,
the mapping consists not in a list of fixed correspondences
but rather in higher-order constraints on what is an appropriate mapping and what is not. Though the metaphor
doesn't tell, for a given event, exactly what slot in the EVENT
schema will correspond to the actor in the ACTION schema,
it does impose constraints.

The difference between metaphors like EVENTS ARE AC-

TIONS and those like LIFE IS A JOURNEY is analogous to the difference between a genus and a species in biology. In a biological taxonomy, each species must have all the characteristics of the genus. Because a genus is defined by a small number of properties at a very high level, it leaves unspecified a great many properties that define a species. A distinction of this sort is needed in the theory of metaphor. We will refer to metaphors like EVENTS ARE ACTIONS as "generic-level metaphors" since they lack specificity in two respects: they do not have fixed source and target domains, and they do not have fixed lists of entities specified in the mapping. We will refer to metaphors like LIFE IS A JOURNEY as "specific-level metaphors," since they are specified in these two ways. We will continue to refer to conventionalized specific-level metaphors as "basic metaphors" when we are not interested in contrasting them with generic-level metaphors.

We can think of this distinction as induced by a corresponding distinction between kinds of schemas. ACTIONS and EVENTS are generic-level schemas, having very little detail filled in, but with a skeletal structure, unlike JOURNEYS and REAPING which have more specific detail. Generic-level metaphors relate generic-level schemas.

There are many possible kinds of information structures which are parameters in generic-level schemas and are therefore available for instantiation by specific-level schemas. Some of the parameters of generic-level structure are these:

— Basic ontological categories: entity, state, event, action, situation, and so on.
— Aspects of beings: attributes, behavior, and so on.
— Event shape: instantaneous or extended; single or repeated; completed or open-ended; preserving, creating, or destroying entities, cyclic or not, that is, with or without fixed stages that end where they begin.
— Causal relations: enabling, resulting in, bringing about, creating, destroying, and so on.
— Image-schemas: bounded regions, paths, forces, links, and so on.
— Modalities: ability, necessity, possibility, obligation, and so on.

Each specific-level schema has such generic-level structure, as well as structure at the lower, specific level. Specific-
level detail is, therefore, of two types: first, there is the detail
that comes from specifying the generic-level parameters;
second, there is lower-level detail. For example, DEATH is
a specific-level schema instance of the generic-level schema
EVENT. As such, it includes the generic-level structure of
EVENT and fills out that structure further by specifying
the values of generic-level parameters. For example, in the
DEATH schema, the event shape is one in which an entity,
over time, *reaches a final state, after which it no longer exists.*
The causal structure of the schema indicates that the passage of time will eventually *result in* that final state being
reached.

To see how this works, consider some examples already
discussed in chapter one in which the event of death is understood in terms of a variety of actions. In each case, the
source-domain action preserves the general shape and causal
structure of the DEATH schema. Death can, thus, be understood metaphorically in terms of reaping, devouring, and
departing, which have the right generic-level structure, but
not so easily in terms of running, making dinner, or filling
the bathtub, which do not.

Though EVENTS ARE ACTIONS permits an open-ended
range of metaphors for a given event such as death, that
range is constrained by the principle of preserving generic-
level structure in the mapping. More specifically, this principle can be stated as follows:
— Preserve the generic level of the target except for what
the metaphor exists explicitly to change.
— Import as much of the generic-level structure of the
source as is consistent with the first condition.
EVENTS ARE ACTIONS exists explicitly to change events to
actions, often by making nonagents into agents, as in "Vitamin E is a great healer" or "Time is a devourer." Here,
general causal structure is preserved, though agency is explicitly changed.

Indeed, we believe that this principle also constrains all
basic metaphors. Though a serious defense of this claim is
well beyond the scope of this book, the idea is important

enough to be worth mentioning. In every basic metaphor, the mapping preserves generic-level structure. In particular, if one takes the portion of the source domain that is mapped and the portion of the target domain it maps onto, they will have the same generic-level structure. For example, in A LIFETIME IS A YEAR, the generic-level structure of the year is a sequence of stages that ends where it began; the same is true of a lifetime. The idea that metaphors preserve generic-level structure is an extremely important idea that we will discuss in chapter four. The preservation of generic-level structure is, we believe, at the heart of metaphorical imagination, whether poetic or ordinary.

The Ordinary Metaphorical Imagination

We have just seen that conventional metaphors can differ in level: metaphors at the specific level have fixed ontological mappings, while metaphors at the generic level guide but do not precisely specify the ontological mappings. In fact, conventional metaphors can differ along a number of other dimensions as well. One of these is the degree to which a given metaphor is founded on our everyday experience and commonplace knowledge. For example, in our everyday experience we constantly encounter cases where an increase in substance (e.g., pouring more water in a glass) increases the height of the substance (e.g., the level of the water in the glass). This provides us with a strong experiential basis for the basic metaphor MORE IS UP, which we use in expressions like "Prices went up," "Turn the radio up," "The market hit bottom," and many others. The strength of the experiential basis for this metaphor explains many things: why the source domain of verticality is paired in a metaphor with the target domain of quantity; why MORE is paired with UP and not with DOWN, and why this metaphor can be learned spontaneously, without being taught.

PURPOSES ARE DESTINATIONS has almost as strong a grounding in everyday experience. Regularly, throughout each day, the achievement of certain purposes requires going to a certain location, as in going to get a glass of water. Here, as in MORE IS UP, we regularly experience the source and the target domains together, with correspondences in our experience which parallel those in the metaphor. When we have many purposes, planning the achievement of those purposes often requires that they be mapped onto a time line. And as we move toward destinations in space we move toward purposes in time.

Metaphors may be grounded not only in recurrent direct experience but also in knowledge. Sexually active people may find that the LUST IS HEAT metaphor, which underlies phrases like "Their lovemaking reached a feverish pitch," coheres with their daily experience. But others may find that this metaphor coheres with their knowledge of sex, which is communicated to them by their cultures. That knowledge is that sex involves physical exertion, and that physical exertion produces heat. For such individuals, the metaphor has no grounding in their experience but has a strong grounding in their commonplace knowledge.

On the other hand, there are basic metaphors with a very different kind of grounding in experience and commonplace knowledge. An example is PEOPLE ARE PLANTS. Youthful vigor and the blossoming of plants do not occur in one-to-one correspondence. Rather, they are both instances of the same process that occurs in all higher-level organisms: flourishing and maturation prior to reproduction. Thus, it is not the case for PEOPLE ARE PLANTS that we have direct experience that connects the source and target domains as we do for MORE IS UP or PURPOSES ARE DESTINATIONS. Nor is it the case that we have strong commonplace knowledge connecting the stages of a plant life and a human life. Nonetheless, this basic metaphor is powerful for us in making sense of our lives, and consequently it is used unconsciously and automatically at the conceptual level and is conventionalized in everyday expressions such as "He withered away."

Thus, basic metaphors vary in the degree to which they have a grounding in experience or cohere with commonplace knowledge. To the extent that a basic metaphor used in poetry is experientially grounded, it draws power from the fundamental nature of those experiences.

Another dimension along which basic metaphors may

differ is their degree of cognitive indispensability. For example, so much of our cognition involves the basic metaphor STATES ARE LOCATIONS that it is difficult to imagine what our cognition would be like without it. For example, consider a state like depression. We speak very naturally of "getting through a depression" or having "sunk into a depression" or "getting out of a depression" or of "going from one depression to the next."

Another basic metaphor indispensable to the way we think about ourselves and our lives is PURPOSES ARE DESTINATIONS. What would it mean to think without conceiving of goals as things we "aim for" and want to "reach" or of difficulties as things "standing in our way" that we have to "get through" or "get around"? It is hard to imagine.

On the opposite end of this dimension of cognitive indispensability, consider LIFE IS BONDAGE(as in "When we have shuffled off this mortal coil . . . ") or DEATH IS SLEEP (as in "For in this sleep of death what dreams may come?"). For most of us, not having these metaphors as part of our conceptual apparatus would not alter our daily behavior or our daily way of construing the events of our lives.

A perhaps less obvious dimension along which basic metaphors can differ is their degree of structural elaboration at the conceptual level. In the opening of chapter one, we presented a long list of structural connections between the domain of life and the schema for a journey. Among them are DIFFICULTIES IN LIFE ARE IMPEDIMENTS TO TRAVEL, COUNSELORS ARE GUIDES, and PROGRESS IS THE DISTANCE TRAVELED. If we were to include further optional elements (e.g., a vehicle at your disposal corresponds to a life-resource), then the list would have been much longer. At the other end of the scale is the small degree of structural elaboration we find in LIFE IS A FLUID. Here, the person corresponds to the container, life corresponds to the fluid in the container, and the way the fluid leaves the container corresponds to the way life leaves the person. That is the extent of the conventional structural elaboration, though of course an inventive poet might find ways to extend the metaphor.

Coherence among Metaphors

The passages cited in chapter one contain a large number of personifications of time: Time the reaper, Time the devourer, Time the destroyer, Time the runner, and so on. As we saw, these apparently disparate metaphors are structurally similar: all of them involve a change over time. We showed earlier in this chapter that this commonality could be characterized adequately by analyzing all of the personifications as special cases of TIME IS A CHANGER, where the differences arise from additional information in the form of other basic metaphors and commonplace knowledge. Moreover, we saw that TIME IS A CHANGER arises by composition of EVENTS ARE ACTIONS with our commonplace knowledge that things change over time. By virtue of such analyses we can see more precisely how metaphors are related to one another.

Because metaphors can be formed by composition, the relationships among metaphors can be extremely complex. Let us now consider some relationships among metaphors where there is no single basic metaphor that is common to them all. Let us ask what relationships there are among the metaphors A LIFETIME IS A DAY, A LIFETIME IS A YEAR, LIFE IS A FLAME, LIFE IS A FIRE, LIFE IS A PRECIOUS POSSESSION, LIFE IS PRESENCE HERE, and LIFE IS A FLUID.

These are all related to one another through a commonplace theory that the source domain of life is structured in a particular way. This commonplace theory can be factored into two parts, a very general part and an elaboration of it. Let us consider the general part first, that life is a cycle, which ends where it began. It has a structure of three stages: first, we're not alive; second, we are alive; and third, we are dead. Because the target domain of LIFE is structured in this way, it is natural to conceive of it in terms of metaphors whose source domains can have the same three-part structure. First, LIFE IS PRESENCE HERE: before birth, we are absent; during life we are present; and after death we are absent again. Second, LIFE IS A PRECIOUS POSSESSION: first we don't have it; then we have it; then we lose it. Third,

LIFE IS A FLAME : first, a candle is not lit; then it is lit; then
it goes out. These metaphors are related in the sense that
each source domain—presence, possession, and flame—can
be mapped onto this tripartite structure in the target domain. The tripartite structure is not a necessary part of any
of the source domains. For example, one might have a precious possession all one's life and never lose it. Nevertheless,
such a tripartite version of the source domain can be chosen
as a coherent basis for a mapping onto the domain of life.
In such cases, the structure of the target domain constrains
the choice of source domain-structure.

Another kind of coherence among metaphors can be seen
in LIFE IS A FLAME, which is a composite of LIFE IS LIGHT
and LIFE IS HEAT. The LIFE IS LIGHT metaphor views death
as darkness, and the LIFE IS HEAT metaphor views death as
cold. Each of these has a strong experiential grounding.
People who are alive are warm, and people who are dead
are cold. People who are alive are typically active during
daylight and inactive during darkness. Plants derive life
from sunlight and die in sustained darkness. Also, there is
a common correlation between light and heat, because in
our daily experience, light sources almost always emit heat
as well.

These two metaphors are extremely basic and extremely
general. Though each is fairly simple in itself, they form
composites with an elaborated version of the commonplace
theory of life as a cycle: at birth, we are relatively powerless;
we grow to our greatest power at maturity, then decline to
powerlessness again at extreme old age. Schematically, this
provides a concept of a life cycle that not only ends where
it begins but also has stages of waxing and then waning
power. LIFE IS LIGHT and LIFE IS HEAT metaphorically fill
out this elaborated cognitive model of the life cycle by using
existing knowledge about the patterns of light and heat to
characterize the nature of that power, metaphorically. The
result is the composite metaphor, LIFE IS A CYCLE OF THE
WAXING AND WANING OF LIGHT AND HEAT.

This extremely general composite metaphor gets filled
out with specific instances in which the source domain in-

cludes a cycle of the waxing and waning of light and heat which ends where it began. What results is a number of much more specific metaphors:

> A LIFETIME IS A YEAR: The year, beginning at the end of winter, grows in intensity of light and heat until full summer, and then the intensity of light and heat declines through fall and winter, to end where it began.

> A LIFETIME IS A DAY: The day, beginning at dawn, has ever stronger light and heat until midday, at which point the intensity of light and heat declines through afternoon, dusk, and night, to end where it began.

> LIFE IS A FIRE: A fire begins slowly, then blazes up, burns steadily, then burns down to embers among the ashes, and finally goes out.

Given this analysis, the relationship among these metaphors becomes clear. They are all instances of the more general composite metaphor of life as a waxing and waning cycle of heat and light. As such they share both LIFE IS LIGHT and LIFE IS HEAT. Given the structure of their source domains, a year, a day, and a fire map naturally onto the structure of life as conceived of as an analogously structured cycle.

The case is rather different with LIFE IS A FLUID, which shows up in expressions like "she's bursting with life," "he's brimming with vim and vigor," and "the life seems to have drained out of him." The portion of the target domain that this metaphor maps onto is not the lifespan but rather the power or vitality evident in the living person. In the metaphor, the fluid maps onto life, the body maps onto the container, and the extent of one's vital powers corresponds to the amount of fluid in the body. At full maturity, we are brimming, and as we reach old age, the life drains out until we dry up. This fits the second half of the conception of life as a waxing-waning cycle: it covers only the waning from full power gradually to death.

Sometimes metaphors are related to one another not because they are special cases of some more general metaphor, or because they map onto the same target structure, but because they have the same grounding in everyday experience or commonplace knowledge. For example, consider the metaphors DEATH IS NIGHT (from A LIFETIME IS A DAY), DEATH IS COLD (from LIFE IS HEAT), DEATH IS DARKNESS (from LIFE IS LIGHT), DEATH IS SLEEP, and DEATH IS REST. They are related by virtue of commonplace knowledge that links their source and target domains: typically, night is cold and dark, people sleep at night, and sleep is rest. Furthermore, dead people are cold, as is night, and are immobile, as if at rest. Thus, night, dark, cold, sleep, and rest are correlated with one another in our commonplace knowledge. It is this correlation that makes the metaphors coherent with one another and accounts for the relationship we sense between them.

The coherence among metaphors is a major source of the power of poetry. By forming a composition of several basic metaphors, a poet draws upon the grounding of those metaphors in common experience and knowledge. When that experience and knowledge cohere, the metaphors seem all the more natural and compelling. Complex metaphors grip us partly because they awake in us the experience and knowledge that form the grounding of those metaphors, partly because they make the coherence of that experience and knowledge resonate, and partly because they lead us to form new coherences in what we know and experience.

Image Metaphors

Not all metaphors map conceptual structures onto other conceptual structures. In addition to the metaphors that unconsciously and automatically organize our ordinary comprehension of the world by mapping concepts onto other concepts, there are also more fleeting metaphors which involve not the mapping of concepts but rather the mapping of images. Consider, for example, this poem from the Indian tradition:

> Now women-rivers
> belted with silver fish
> move unhurried as women in love
> at dawn after a night with their lovers
> (*The Peacock's Egg*, p. 71)

89

Here the the image of the slow, sinuous walk of an Indian woman is mapped onto the image of the slow, sinuous, shimmering flow of a river. The shimmering of a school of fish is imagined as the shimmering of the belt.

Metaphoric image-mappings work in just the same way as all other metaphoric mappings—by mapping the structure of one domain onto the structure of another. But here the domains are mental images. Image structure includes both part-whole structure and attribute structure. In images, part-whole relations are relations such as those between a roof and a house, or between a tombstone and a grave as a whole. Attribute structure includes such things as color, intensity of light, physical shape, curvature, and, for events, aspects of the overall shape, such as continuous versus discrete, open-ended versus completed, repetitive versus not repetitive, brief versus extended. It is the existence of such structure within our conceptual images that permits one image to be mapped onto another by virtue of their common structure.

For example, consider:

My wife . . . whose waist is an hourglass.

This is a superimposition of the image of an hourglass onto the image of a woman's waist by virtue of their common shape. As before, the metaphor is conceptual; it is not in the words themselves. In these cases, the locus of the metaphor is the mental image. Here, we have a mental image of an hourglass and of a woman, and we map the middle of the hourglass onto the waist of the woman. Note that the words do not tell us which part of the hourglass to map onto the waist, or even that it only part of the hourglass shape that corresponds to the waist. The words are prompts for us to perform mapping from one conventional image to another at the conceptual level. Similarly, consider:

His toes were like the keyboard of a spinet.
(Rabelais, "The Descriptions of King Lent," trans.
    J. M. Cohen)

Here too, the words do not tell us that an individual toe corresponds to an individual key on the keyboard. Again, the words are prompts for us to perform a conceptual mapping between conventional mental images. In particular, we map aspects of the part-whole structure of one image onto aspects of the part-whole structure of another. Just as individual keys are parts of the whole keyboard, so individual toes are parts of the whole foot.

Image-mapping can involve more than mapping physical part-whole relationships. For example, the water line of a river may drop slowly and that slowness is part of the dynamic image, which may be mapped onto the removal of clothing:

> Slowly slowly rivers in autumn show
> sand banks
> bashful in first love woman
> showing thighs
> (*The Peacock's Egg*, p. 69)

Other attributes are also mapped: the color of the sand bank onto the color of flesh, the quality of light on a wet sand bank onto the reflectiveness of skin, the light grazing of the water's touch receding down the bank onto the light grazing of the clothing along the skin. Notice that the words do not tell us that any clothing is involved. We get that from conventional mental images. Part-whole structure is also mapped in this example. The water covers the hidden part of the bank just as the clothing covers the hidden part of the body.

The proliferation of detail in the images limits image-mappings to highly specific cases. That is why we refer to them as "one-shot." We will contrast these below with image-schema mappings, where there is no rich imagistic detail. They also contrast with robust conceptual mappings such as LIFE IS A JOURNEY, where rich knowledge and rich inferential structure are mapped from the domain of journeys onto life. One-shot image-mappings characteristically do not involve the mapping of such rich knowledge and inferential structure. Moreover, LIFE IS A JOURNEY is used unconsciously and automatically over and over again in reasoning about our lives. But one-shot image-mappings are not involved in daily reasoning.

Image-metaphors can trigger and reinforce metaphors that map conceptual knowledge and inferential structure. For example, in chapter one we saw image-mappings of a choir loft onto a tree and a tree onto a man. Mapping a tree onto a man can trigger the PEOPLE ARE PLANTS metaphor, which, as we saw, maps knowledge and inferences from the domain of plants onto the domain of people.

Such mapping of one image onto another can lead us to map knowledge about the first image onto knowledge about the second. Consider this example from the Navaho:

> My horse with a mane made of short rainbows.[3]

The structure of a rainbow, its band of curved lines, for example, is mapped onto an arc of curved hair, and many rainbows onto many such arcs on the horse's mane. Such image-mapping prompts us to map our evaluation of the source domain onto the target. We know that rainbows are beautiful, special, inspiring, larger than life, almost mystic, and that seeing them makes us happy and awestruck. This knowledge is mapped onto what we know of the horse: it too is awe-inspiring, beautiful, larger than life, almost mystic. This line comes from a poem containing a series of such image-mappings:

> My horse with a hoof like a striped agate,
> with his fetlock like a fine eagle plume:
> my horse whose legs are like quick lightning
> whose body is an eagle-plumed arrow:
> my horse whose tail is like a trailing black cloud.

The image-mappings we have considered so far lead us to map conventional knowledge about the source-domain image onto the target domain in ways that extend but do not disturb what we know of the target domain. A poet may, however, wish to break our expectations about the image correspondence and disturb what we think we know about the target domain. For example, a surrealist poem might

---

[3] Tell Kia ahni, "War God's Horse Song I," interpreted by Louis Watchman, in Jerome Rothenberg, ed., *Technicians of the Sacred* (Berkeley and Los Angeles: University of California Press, 1985), p. 40.

begin with a conventional image-mapping and then, in subsequent image-mappings, depart from our ordinary techniques for mapping structure onto structure, with the
purpose of making us explore afresh the ways we see and
think. Consider, for example, David Antin's translation of
the beginning of André Breton's "Free Union."

> My wife whose hair is a brush fire
> Whose thoughts are summer lightning
> Whose waist is an hourglass
> Whose waist is the waist of an otter caught in the
>   teeth of a tiger
> Whose mouth is a bright cockade with the fragrance
>   of a star of the first magnitude
> Whose teeth leave prints like the tracks of white mice
>   over snow
> Whose tongue is made out of amber and polished
>   glass
> Whose tongue is a stabbed wafer

As before, these words are prompts for us to perform mappings at the conceptual level between mental images. Since
these mappings are not conventional, different readers commonly achieve different readings of surrealist poetry. Consider the mapping between hair and a brush fire. How
might we accomplish a mapping when we are given merely
the source image and the target image and none of the details of the mapping? We might for example see the general
physical outline of hair with tendrils as corresponding to
flickering peaks and wisps of flame. Or we might see the
dancing play of sunlight glistening off the hair as corresponding to the skittering of flame through the brush and,
furthermore, the actual strands of hair as corresponding to
plant shoots ablaze in the brush. We might map the color
of a fire onto the wife's hair, making her a redhead. Such
possible mappings of image-structure onto image-structure
might lead us to explore possible knowledge mappings. For
example, brush fires are notoriously difficult to control and
therefore dangerous. They break out without warning and
flare up quickly. How might we map this knowledge onto
the wife's hair? We might, for instance, construe the volatile

image of her hair as an outward manifestation of her mind—
its uncontrollability, spontaneity, and volatility. This might
make her not only dangerous but also exciting. Why the
speaker (or reader) sees the wife this way is an open question. The answers we have heard range from love to awe to
misogyny.

So far, we have discussed cases where a source image is
mapped onto a target domain which *contains* an image. A
source image might also be mapped onto a target domain
in order to *create* an image in the target domain. For example, the phrase "thoughts are summer lightning" maps
our image of summer lightning onto the domain of thought,
which is abstract and therefore does not inherently contain an image. This mapping creates for us an image of a
thought as a particularly powerful lightning bolt. If this
mapping creates an image for us, why should it seem so
natural? Why should it seem appropriate in some intuitive
sense that thought could be lightning? The explanation lies
in knowledge we have of the source and target domains. For
example, we know that lightning illuminates and, metaphorically, through the metaphor that insight is illumi-
nation, that thoughts illuminate. We know that insights
illuminate by virtue of the basic UNDERSTANDING IS SEE-
ING metaphor: what enables you to see is metaphorically
what enables you to understand. But not just any thought
can be lightning. Lightning is instantaneous, and thoughts
that are instantaneous do not occur as part of a logical pro-
gression. They are flashes of intuition which may seem to
come from nowhere. And just as lightning can have a force,
so ideas can be forceful.

Part of the point of surrealist poetry is to make readers
go through the process of an imaginative construction
in ways that tax our conventional expectations. Take the
line "whose tongue is a stabbed wafer." How might we
go through the process of constructing a mapping, given
merely the source image of a stabbed wafer and the target
image of the wife's tongue? Here readings are likely to
be highly idiosyncratic, which is part of the point of the
poem. Is the tongue a wafer stabbed by something else, per-

haps another tongue during kissing? Is the wafer both the
tongue and the body of Christ? Is the stabbing an act of
love, lust, cruelty, or all three?

We said above that a surrealist poem might take a conventional image-mapping and depart from it. Here, the poet
takes the conventional, easy image-mapping of an hourglass
onto the waist of a woman and instantly follows it with the
mapping between the waist of the wife and the waist of an
otter caught in the teeth of a tiger. How might we construct
a mapping here? First, an otter's waist, which is smooth,
will be made thinner and tighter by the clenching teeth of
the tiger, and will be in writhing motion. We might map
this image structure onto the image of the wife's waist. We
also know something about the situation of the otter. It is
struggling in a life-and-death situation. We might also map
this aspect of struggle and immediacy onto our knowledge
of the wife.

On the basis of these various image-mappings, we might
ultimately come to think of the wife as dangerous, un-
controllable, unpredictable, exciting, erotic, smooth, struggling, endangered, and intense.

Here we have seen how mappings of image-structures can
compose with basic metaphors and result in the mapping
of knowledge. One of the most spectacular compositions
of image-mapping is with the processes of personification
we discussed earlier in this chapter and at various points
throughout chapter one. Until now, we have discussed only
personifications of abstract concepts like death and time,
which do not themselves contain image-structures. However, in personifying something concrete which already contains an image, we may superimpose the image of a person
on the image of that thing. Consider Blake's personification
of a sunflower:

> Ah Sun-flower! weary of time,
> Who countest the steps of the Sun,
> Seeking after that sweet golden clime
> Where the traveller's journey is done:
>
> Where the Youth pined away with desire,
> And the pale Virgin shrouded in snow

Arise from their graves and aspire,
Where my Sun-flower wishes to go.
("Ah! Sun-flower")

The by-now familiar processes of personification are at work here. First, the sun's crossing the sky is a natural event, and the sunflower's phototropic tracking of the sun is also a natural event. Through EVENTS ARE ACTIONS, these are conceived of metaphorically as actions with agents. The sun is an agent whose action is walking. The sunflower is an agent whose action is to count, and hence to follow, the steps of the sun. The sunflower further acts by seeking the west. Through the metaphor A LIFETIME IS A DAY, the west is metaphorically conceived of as associated with death. And therefore the sunflower is seeking, metaphorically, death and its afterlife. Such metaphoric processes we have seen many times by now.

But here, because the sunflower is a concrete physical entity, we have an image of it. Therefore, personifying the sunflower composes with mapping the image of a person onto the image of the sunflower: the face of the person corresponds to the "face" of the sunflower; the orientation of the face of a person looking at the sun corresponds the orientation of the sunflower's face; the body of the person corresponds to the stem of the sunflower; the place where the person is standing corresponds to the place where the sunflower is planted.

Similarly, because we have an image of the sun, the personification of the sun composes with mapping the image of a person onto the image of the sun. The face of the person corresponds to the circle of the sun. One might extend this image-mapping, to give the sun legs to walk with along the path of his ecliptic.

The apparent simplicity of the Blake poem, a simplicity almost innocent, naive, and childlike, involves at the conceptual level a highly elaborate composition of metaphoric processes. Thus, we are led again to consider how things apparently obvious to us involve highly imaginative conceptual connections, extensions, and compositions.

Image Schemas

It seems obvious that someone unconscious or asleep is "out"; that a machine or computer that is not working is "down"; that communication is "across." It may be hard ever to notice that any metaphoric work is done in these cases at all. When we discussed Shakespeare's "Out, out, brief candle" and "Put out the light, and then put out the light" as references to death, we explained them as deriving from the metaphor LIFE IS A FLAME. But we did not discuss why, independent of this metaphor, death is widely and generally understood as being "out."

What do we know about "out"? We know that the basic meaning of "out" is being exterior to a bounded space which is regarded as having an interior. If a house is the bounded region, one may go *out* of the house and into the garage. If land is taken as the bounded region, one may go *out* to sea. If wakefulness is seen as a bounded region (through the metaphor STATES ARE LOCATIONS), one may metaphorically pass *out*. If alertness is the bounded region, one may space *out*, zone *out*, tune *out*, or veg *out*. Since life is regarded as presence here, bounded by birth and death, one may be metaphorically snuffed *out*, rubbed *out*, taken *out*, and so on.

A bounded space with an interior and an exterior is an image, but an extremely skeletal and schematic image. Sometimes we map this image-schema onto other images, such as our relatively rich image of a house, a garage, or the outline of a country on a map. But we can also map this image-schema onto abstract target domains that themselves do not inherently contain images, such as wakefulness, alertness, and living.

We have many such image-schemas that we use in just the same ways. In addition to the schema of a bounded space, we have image-schemas of a path, of contact, and of human orientations like up-down, front-back, and center-periphery. When we understand a scene, we naturally structure it in terms of such elementary image-schemas. Prepositions are the means English has for expressing these schematic spatial relations. Because of the many metaphors that allow abstract concepts to be understood in terms of physical objects and spatial relations, we can use these elementary image-schemas to structure abstract domains, as we do in "in love," "out of power," and so on.

We are almost in a position to explain the occurrence of "out" in "Out, out, brief candle." Two elements of the explanation are in place. First, the LIFE IS LIGHT and LIFE IS HEAT metaphors link the flame of the candle with life and the lack of it with death. Second, the LIFE IS PRESENCE HERE metaphor takes life as a bounded region that living beings are in. As Twain said, he "came in" with Halley's comet and would "go out" with it. Death is therefore "out."

Finally, we need to explain why, when a light source becomes nonfunctional, the light is conceptualized as "going out." This is not special to light sources. Nonfunctionality, in general, is conceptualized as being *out* (of the center of functional interaction). Thus, people who are nonfunctional are said to "zone out," be "zonked out," or be "out of it"; and when a machine ceases functioning, it is said to be "out of order" or "out of commission" or to have "conked out." Thus, it is not just candles that are "out," but also generators, telephone service, and so on. Thus, "Out, out, brief candle" is metaphorically coherent in two ways: not only do the LIFE IS LIGHT and LIFE IS HEAT metaphors link the lack of flame with death, but moreover both the nonfunctionality of a light source and death are oriented *out*. The "going" of "going out" is straightforward: since STATES ARE LOCATIONS, changes of state are changes of location, that is, motions. Motion away from where "we" normally are is expressed as "going."

Because image-schemas can be used to structure both physical scenes and abstract domains, Auden can use one image-schema to connect the image of a leaking teacup with the domain of life and death:

> The glacier knocks in the cupboard,
> The desert sighs in the bed,
> And the crack in the tea-cup opens
> A lane to the land of the dead.
> ("As I Walked Out One Evening")

The teacup is understood in terms of the bounded-space schema, with the fluid in the bounded-space within the tea-cup. Life is also understood in terms of the bounded space schema, with the vital fluids of life inside the body, which is a bounded space. In terms of this schema, the crack in the teacup lets the fluid run out, forming a stream, which is an instance of the PATH image-schema. Correspondingly, in the LIFE IS A FLUID metaphor, the metaphoric fluid drains out, forming a path.

The DEATH IS DEPARTURE metaphor is also structured by this complex image-schema: a departure originates at the edge of a bounded space and proceeds along a path, and metaphorically death as departure originates at the edge of the bounded space of life and proceeds along a metaphoric path to a final destination, the land of the dead. Thus, Au-den connects LIFE IS A FLUID with DEATH IS DEPARTURE via the overlapping image-schemas: the stream of the fluid overlaps with the lane to the land of the dead, since both are paths originating in bounded spaces.

It is important to distinguish image-metaphors from im-age-schema metaphors. Image-metaphors map rich mental images onto other rich mental images. They are one-shot metaphors, relating one rich image with one other rich im-age. Image-schemas, as their name suggests, are not rich mental images; they are instead very general structures, like bounded regions, paths, centers (as opposed to peripher-ies), and so on. The spatial senses of prepositions tend to be defined in terms of image-schemas (e.g., *in, out, to, from, along,* and so on).

In physical domains, image-schemas have two roles. First, they provide structure for rich mental images. It is by virtue of such structure that one rich mental image can be mapped onto another: for instance, the stream of fluid coming from the cup can map onto the lane to the land of the dead be-cause they share the image-schema structure of a path ema-nating from a bounded space. Second, image-schemas have an internal logic that permits spatial reasoning. For ex-ample, if an item x is in a bounded space A, and A is in a bounded space B, then x is in B.

When metaphors map spatial domains onto nonspatial,

abstract domains, the image-schemas and their attendant logic are preserved by the mappings. Thus, bounded regions map onto bounded regions, paths map onto paths, and so on. Correspondingly, the spatial logic of the image-schemas is preserved by metaphorical mappings and becomes abstract logic in the nonspatial target domains. For example, conceptual categories are metaphorically understood as bounded spaces, and so the logic of bounded spaces applies to conceptual categories: if item x is in category A and A is in category B, then x is in B. Moreover, many of the nonspatial uses of prepositions arise by such metaphors. Thus, the proposition "in" is used for categories as well as bounded spaces, and, as we saw, "out" is used both for nonfunctionality and nonexistence. Let us now consider the implications of these properties of image-schemas.

Metonymy

Let us now turn to another aspect of the use of the word "lane" in the Auden poem. A lane is part of a schema for traveling. The use of "lane" and "to" evokes not only the concept of a lane but also the entire schema for motion toward a destination. Such an evocation of an entire schema via the mention of a part of that schema is one kind of *metonymy*.

Yeats uses this form of metonymy in "That The Night Come":

> She lived in storm and strife,
> Her soul had such desire
> For what proud death may bring
> That it could not endure
> The common good of life,
> But lived as 'twere a king
> That packed his marriage day
> With banneret and pennon,
> Trumpet and kettledrum,
> And the outrageous cannon,
> To bundle time away
> That the night come.

Banneret and pennon, trumpet and kettledrum, and the outrageous cannon—these are props of an aristocratic state

100

ceremony, and they are also props of war. On the most obvious reading, the props evoke the state ceremony as a whole. Since the props also evoke a schema for war, the metonymy provides an extended reading wherein the props of war at a marriage indicate such a consuming concern with war that it pervades even the domestic sphere. Here, using a metonymy does important poetic work since it can evoke more than one schema.

There is a second variety of metonymy in which one element of a schema stands not for the whole schema but for some other element of the schema. Consider this passage from Yeats's "The Second Coming":

> . . . but now I know
> That twenty centuries of stony sleep
> Were vexed to nightmare by a rocking cradle . . .

Here, the rocking cradle stands for the baby it contains, namely Christ. Such a metonymy is referential in nature; by referring to the cradle, the poet can refer to Christ.

But why use a metonymy at all? Why not just say "Christ"? One reason is that the passage occurs in a poem about historical cycles, focusing on the Second Coming. The poem contains many images of cycles, from "Turning and turning in the widening gyre / The falcon cannot hear the falconer," to tides, to "the darkness drops again," to "what rough beast, its hour come round at last." Even the title, "The Second Coming," suggests images of cyclic return. Thus the mention of the repetitive rocking of the cradle does more than simply refer to Christ—it connects the coming of Christ with the cyclic nature of events. The rocking cradle also can evoke some agent doing the rocking, and we may connect this agent with the cosmic force or forces that bring about the historical cycles. Thus, there is an important poetic effect, above and beyond reference, arising from the use of metonymy in this passage.

Sometimes two referential metonymies can occur in the same clause and produce a complex interaction. Let us look again to Yeats, this time to a passage from "The Tower":

> It seems that I must bid the Muse go pack,
> Choose Plato and Plotinus for a friend

Until imagination, ear and eye,
Can be content with argument . . .

Here we have four metonymies in four lines. First take "bid the Muse go pack." Given the cultural model in which poets can only write with the inspiration of a Muse, telling the Muse to pack evokes a scenario in which the Muse is made to leave and as a result the poet can no longer write. Bidding the Muse go pack thus stands metonymically for giving up writing poetry. Second, "ear and eye" stand for the faculties of hearing and vision. The third and fourth cases are in the phrase "choose Plato and Plotinus for a friend." The commonly assumed scenario for friendship includes friends spending time together. Thus, choosing Plato and Plotinus for a friend stands for spending time with them. Of course, since they are long dead, one cannot literally do that. Here a common metonymy— AUTHOR FOR WORKS— comes into play; the poet is to spend time with their works, not with them in person.

Metonymy can operate either on whole clauses or on individual noun phrases within a clause. Sometimes the reading one gets depends on the metonymy one selects. Consider:

> The monk stares at
> her navel
> and she at the moon his face
> the crows steal
> both their
> spoon and their bowl
> (*The Peacock's Egg*, p. 41)

The poem is rich in sexual imagery. It evokes four image-metaphors: the image of the moon maps on the face of the monk; the image of the woman's navel maps onto female genitalia; and the spoon and bowl map onto male and female genitalia. These image-metaphors make possible various metonymies, and the choice of metonymies leads to two quite different readings.

On the first reading, there is an instance of the EFFECT FOR CAUSE metonymy, in which the theft of the spoon and the bowl stands for its cause, the total obliviousness of the monk and the woman to anything but each other. This reading stresses the overwhelmingly strong sensual nature of the encounter and leaves us with the suggestion that the monk's vows of celibacy may be forgotten as well.

On the second reading, there is a complex interaction of metaphor and metonymy. First, the crow symbolizes death. It does so in two ways. By metonymy alone, the crow (a scavenger that feeds on dead animals) evokes, and stands for, death. And by the DEATH IS DARKNESS metaphor, together with the PART FOR WHOLE metonymy, the blackness of the crow stands for death in another way. Next, the spoon and bowl, mapped by image-metaphors onto male and female genitalia, stand metonymically for sexual vitality. Finally, by EVENTS ARE ACTIONS and LIFE IS A PRECIOUS POSSESSION, death steals their sexual vitality. The suggestion is that the meditative life has robbed the monk of his sexuality.

Metonymy and metaphor are sometimes confused because each is a connection between two things. But the connections are very different:

— In *metaphor*, there are two conceptual domains, and one is understood in terms of the other.
— In *metaphor*, a whole schematic structure (with two or more entities) is mapped onto another whole schematic structure.
— In *metaphor*, the logic of the source-domain structure is mapped onto the logic of the target-domain structure.

None of this is true in metonymy.

— *Metonymy* involves only one conceptual domain. A metonymic mapping occurs within a single domain, not across domains.
— *Metonymy* is used primarily for reference: via metonymy, one can refer to one entity in a schema by referring to another entity in the same schema.
— In *metonymy*, one entity in a schema is taken as standing for one other entity in the same schema, or for the schema as a whole.

Metaphor and metonymy do have some things in common.

— Both are conceptual in nature.
— Both are mappings.

— Both can be conventionalized, that is, made part of our everyday conceptual system, and thus used automatically, effortlessly, and without conscious awareness.

— In both, linguistic expressions that name source elements of the mapping typically also name target elements. That is, both are means of extending the linguistic resources of a language.

Because of these similarities, they are often confused. For this reason, it is important to keep all the differences in mind.

Interactions of Metonymy with Metaphor

One of the reasons that metaphor and metonymy are sometimes confused is that they can interact in complex ways to yield composites. Consider Old Norse kennings, which are typically composites of metonymies and image-metaphors. Here is an example:

> The winter passer of the current
> waded firmly through the snowdrifts of the fjord-
>   snake.
>
> The bear of the masthead knobs
> leapt over the peaks of the whale house.
>
> The bear of the high sea
> went forward on old tracks of sea skis.
>
> The storm-upright bear of the prop
> broke through the crashing fetter of low-lying rocks.
> (Markús Skeggjason)

This a passage about a sea voyage. Each couplet describes a stage of the voyage, and each consists of a simple sentence describing the ship, how it sailed, and what the seas were like at that stage of the voyage. In each couplet, the sturdy Norse ship, lumbering through icy northern seas, is described via an image-metaphor as a bear moving over a wintry terrain.

In the first couplet, "winter passer" refers metaphorically to a bear who has hibernated through at least one winter, that is, a mature bear. "Current" metonymically evokes the sea. Thus, "the winter passer of the current," via two occurrences of metonymy, yields "the bear of the sea." This gives rise to an image-metaphor, in which the sea is the target domain and the image of a mature bear is mapped onto the image of a sturdy, lumbering ship. Correspondingly, our salient knowledge of northern bears is metaphorically mapped onto knowledge about the ship: it is strong, aggressive, and undaunted by the weather. "The snowdrifts of the fjord-snake" is understood via two image-metaphors: snowdrifts on land map onto ice floes in the fjord, which is shaped like a snake. A further image-metaphor maps the wading of the bear onto the careful rowing of the ship through the snaky, floe-filled fjord, with the bear's steps into the drifts mapping onto the dipping of the oars into the water.

In the second couplet, "masthead knobs" refers directly to the knobs on the mastheads of such ships. By metonymy, the masthead knobs evoke the ship's masts, and hence the ship with sails flying. The "of" in "the bear of the masthead knobs" is an approximate English translation of an Old Norse grammatical form, the genitive case, which can be used "appositively" in a way that English "of" is not widely used today. The result has a meaning like "the bear, which is something having masthead knobs." The result again is an image-metaphor mapping the bear onto the ship, this time the ship under sail. "The peaks of the whale house" is also interpreted via an image-metaphor: the whale house is the open sea, where the whales live, and the image of roof peaks of a house are mapped onto the peaks of the waves. In addition, the image of a bear jumping over peaks is mapped onto an image of the ship under sail riding over the peaks of the waves on the open sea.

In the third couplet, "the bear of the high sea" again refers to the ship. "Old tracks of sea skis" evokes both an image of well-worn cross-country skiing trails, mapping them onto the domain of the sea, to yield well traveled sea lanes. Here the ship is on the open sea, traveling the common sea lanes.

In the last couplet, "the prop" refers to the scaffolding holding a ship upright in dry dock, and that image is mapped onto the image of the ship "storm-upright" in rough seas. The "fetter of the low-lying rocks" refers to the chain of rocks surrounding the coast of Norway, the destination of the ship. Again there is an image-mapping of a chain onto the the chain of rocks. "Crashing" metonymically evokes the image and sound of waves against the rocks. The resulting image of "The storm-upright bear of the prop / broke through the crashing fetter of low-lying rocks" is one in which the ship, upright in the crashing waves, passes through the chain of rocks off the Norwegian coast.

Kennings are an extreme example of how metaphor and metonymy can interact to form a unified interpretation. What makes kennings special, from our point of view, is the complexity of composition that they show—the sheer density of image-metaphor and metonymy.

All Reading Is Reading In

Words, as we have seen, evoke schemas. Just how does a word evoke a schema? Consider the words "bloom," "traveler," and "ashes." The word "bloom" is meaningful only as defined relative to plants; "traveler" is meaningful only as defined relative to journeys; and "ashes" is meaningful only as defined relative to a fire. Our knowledge about plants, journeys, and fires is organized schematically in such a way that blooms, travelers, and ashes are elements of that knowledge organization; and therefore the words "bloom," "traveler," and "ashes," which denote those elements, evoke the full schemas for plants, journeys, and fires.

Because words can evoke schemas, and metaphors map schemas into other schemas, words can prompt a metaphorical understanding. Take the word "flame," in a sentence like "The flame finally went out." It evokes the schema for fire, and thus we can take it merely to mean that the fire, say in the stove or fireplace, went out. But since the schema for fire is also the source domain for two ordinary conceptual metaphors, LIFE IS FIRE and LOVE IS FIRE, it can evoke the application of either of those metaphors. Thus, we can understand "The flame finally went out" metaphorically as meaning either that someone died or that the emotion that sustained a love affair has disappeared.

In many cases, the ability of a word to evoke a conceptual metaphor is conventionalized in the language. Take the ex-

pression "old flame," which evokes the LOVE IS FIRE metaphor in a conventional way. It is part of the lexicon of
English. It uses the word "flame," which belongs to the
source domain of fire; when conventionally combined with
"old," it only denotes a former lover, that is, an element of
the target domain of love. There are other cases, where
a single word can conventionally evoke either a source-
domain element or a target-domain element. Take a word
like "withered," which can refer either to a plant or to a
person, since it conventionally picks out elements of both
the source and target domains of PEOPLE ARE PLANTS. The
sense of "withered" that applies to people is commonly
called a *metaphoric extension* of the central sense of "withered," which applies to plants. This metaphoric extension
of "withered" is fully conventional in our language, by
which we mean that it is routine and unconscious.

A poet can use words to evoke a conceptual metaphor,
even though they are not automatically and routinely used
for that purpose. For example, when Dickinson says, "Because I could not stop for Death / He kindly stopped for
me," she is evoking with unusual words the same DEATH IS
DEPARTURE metaphor we routinely evoke with the conventional words "pass away."

It is common to hear a phrase like "I could not stop for
Death" called a "metaphor," with the words themselves seen
as constituting the metaphor. As common as it is to do so,
it can be misleading to speak of a sequence of words as being a metaphor. Linguistic expressions—mere sequences of
words—are not metaphors in themselves. Metaphors are
conceptual mappings. They are a matter of thought, not
merely language. Part of the confusion arises because the
words that conventionally express a source-domain concept
can, in the typical case, also be used to express the corresponding target-domain concept, as when "withered" is applied both to plants and to people.

Throughout this book we have been careful to keep
separate linguistic expressions and the concepts that they
express. By noting which words, or sequences of words, conventionally express source-domain concepts, we have been

able to chart the regularities by which source-domain concepts are mapped onto target-domain concepts, and hence to characterize the structure of metaphorical mappings.

Having discussed the nature of metonymy, we are now in a position to discuss the major source of the confusion over the use of the term "metaphor." There is a general metonymy whereby WORDS STAND FOR THE CONCEPTS THEY EXPRESS. It is as general and automatic a metonymy as there is, since in the use of language, words *do* stand for the concepts they express. However, this fact about the use of language is distinct from the metonymy itself. The metonymy can be seen in expressions such as "That is a self-contradictory utterance." Strictly speaking, what one utters are sequences of sounds. Sequences of sounds, in themselves, do not have logical properties and so cannot be self-contradictory. But, by metonymy, we understand "utterance" in "That is a self-contradictory utterance" as referring to the conceptual content expressed by the utterance, and it is that conceptual content that is being claimed to be self-contradictory. Similarly, in a sentence like "Those are foolish words," the words are taken as referring, via metonymy, to the concept expressed by the words, which are being called foolish.

The word "metaphor" itself is subject to the metonymy that WORDS STAND FOR THE CONCEPTS THEY EXPRESS. That is, because of the existence of this metonymy in our conceptual system, "metaphor" can refer both to a conceptual mapping across domains and to the words expressing such a mapping. When the distinction between the words and their conceptual content is clear, there is no harm in using this metonymy, which is after all part of the structure of our language, and using the term "metaphor" to denote the words that express a conceptual metaphor.

The confusion arises when the metonymy goes unnoticed and no distinction is made between the words in themselves and concepts they express. This is especially pernicious in the case of metaphor, because there, words can express not one concept but two or more—the source-domain concept and any metaphorical concepts that it maps onto.

A related confusion arises in literary studies. It is the idea that the meaning of a poem or other literary work resides in the words themselves. Words are sound sequences that conventionally express concepts that are within conceptual schemas. Consequently, words typically evoke conceptual schemas beyond the part of the schema that the word designates. Thus, "reaper" evokes the entire schema for plant cultivation. That is, words evoke in the mind much more than they strictly designate. What is meaningful are not the words, the mere sound sequences spoken or letter sequences on a page, but the conceptual content that the words evoke. Meanings are thus in people's minds, not in the words on the page.

In the case of metaphor, this distinction is all the more important because people have, as part of their normal conceptual systems, a wealth of conceptual metaphors that they use to make sense of their experience. These metaphors, like other conceptual content, reside in people's minds, not on any pages or in any sounds. Many meanings are conventional and shared, and these limit what a literary work can mean to someone. Literary works, for this reason, can't mean just anything. But, because what is meaningful is in the mind, not in the words, there is an enormous range of possibilities open for reasonable interpretation of a literary work.

When a reader gives a highly unusual or idiosyncratic construal of a poem, he is sometimes accused of "reading meanings into" the poem that are not "really there." But, because of the nature of language, all reading is reading in. Even if one sticks to the conventional, shared meanings of the words, one will necessarily be evoking all of the knowledge in the schemas in which those words are defined. And in using one's natural capacity for metaphorical understanding, one will necessarily be engaging in an activity of construal. All reading involves construal.

Linguists have discovered that no two speakers speak exactly the same language. Each speaker of a language differs from all others in details of grammar, of word meaning, and of conceptual structure.

Literary works, and poems in particular, are open to

widely varying construals. For any given person, some construals will seem more natural than others, and those are the
ones that are often ascribed to the intention of the poet.
But if we actually talk to contemporary poets about their
poems, we find that the poet's most natural construals may
not be our own. That is normal, inevitable, and part of what
makes poetry valuable and of lasting interest. Poems stand
on their own. They evoke our construals and those construals are of value, whether they coincide with the author's
or not. That is not to say that literary scholars should not
engage in historical study that attempts to home in on
the author's intended construals, to the extent that they can
be pinned down. But that is a separate enterprise from
what readers normally do when they encounter works of
literature.

Given that all reading involves construal, the question
arises as to what principles govern the nature of construal.
This book attempts to provide such principles in the area of
metaphor.

Traditional Views

To comprehend the power of metaphor, one must understand its nature. We have devoted this chapter to characterizing the nature of metaphor to the best of our abilities. But
our account of the nature of metaphor is by no means the
only one. There are traditional views that conflict with ours,
views that, on the basis of our best evidence, we believe are
mistaken. Indeed, one of the main reasons that we have
bothered to write this book is that we believe that such traditional views are in error. We will devote the remainder of
this chapter to outlining those views and to explaining
where we think they go wrong.

As we see it, there are six fundamental positions that we
consider mistaken. The first, and biggest, mistake concerns
what has been called "literal meaning." The second is to fail
to seek general principles and to focus instead on individual
metaphorical expressions as if each were unique. The third
is a confusion between presently existing conventional metaphors and metaphors that once existed but no longer do,
the so-called "dead" metaphors. The fourth mistake is the

claim that metaphors do not have a source and a target domain, but are merely bidirectional linkages across domains. The fifth mistake is the claim that metaphor resides in linguistic expressions alone and not in conceptual structure. Finally, the sixth mistake is the claim that everything in language and thought is metaphorical, that there are no aspects of language or thought that are not metaphorical.

SEMANTIC AUTONOMY

The theoretical concept of literal meaning depends on the prior notion of semantic autonomy. An expression in a language is semantically autonomous if it is meaningful completely on its own terms. It follows that any expression that is semantically autonomous does not derive any of its meaning from metaphor. Nor does it derive its meaning through other conceptual relationships that stand outside of classical logic, such as metonymy, irony, conversational principles, and so on.

Conceptual autonomy. There are two variants of the notion of semantic autonomy. The first, conceptual autonomy, assumes that there are concepts and that words and phrases in a language express concepts. Concepts are cognitive in nature; that is, they are part of human cognition. On this view, it is concepts, not words and phrases, that have meaning. Words and phrases are meaningful only via the concepts they express. Concepts are semantically autonomous if they are meaningful completely on their own terms. The meaning of semantically autonomous concepts is, hence, independent of metaphor, metonymy, conversational principles, and so on. On this view, an expression of a language is semantically autonomous if the concept it expresses is semantically autonomous.

Nonconceptual autonomy. This variant assumes either that there are no such things as concepts, or that concepts play no role in characterizing meaning. It assumes that words and phrases in a language get their meaning via what they designate in the world, not via human cognition. Hence, the meaning of a semantically autonomous linguistic expression is independent of metaphor, metonymy, principles of conversation, and so on. On this view, meaning resides in the relation between words and the world and is independent of human cognition. This variant of the idea of semantic autonomy will become important below when we discuss the No Concepts Position on metaphor. Until then, the distinction between these variants will not matter. The general theory of literal meaning is neutral between them.

GROUNDING

We have argued throughout this book that metaphor is conceptual in nature and that metaphors are mappings from one conceptual domain to another. We have also argued that there are a considerable number of *conventional* metaphors, that is, cross-domain conceptual mappings that are automatic, unconscious, and effortless. Conventional metaphors map conventional concepts in one domain (e.g., journey, night) onto conventional concepts in a completely different domain (e.g., life, death). Thus, at least some aspects of many conventional concepts are understood via metaphor. Among these are our conceptions of life, death, and time.

We began this chapter by asking what is not metaphorical. We considered the concept of a dog and observed that some aspects of that concept are understood without metaphor; for example, physical traits like a dog's legs, nose, and tail are conventionally understood without metaphor, that is, without reference to a completely different conceptual domain. Thus, a dog's tail is conventionally understood nonmetaphorically, although we could understand it via a novel image-metaphor as a flag the dog waves. On the other hand, at least one aspect of the conventional concept of a dog is understood via metaphor, namely, a dog's loyalty, which is understood in terms of a human character trait.

The moral is that we cannot always speak of *all* of a given conventional concept as being understood either via conventional metaphor or without conventional metaphor. When a concept has a complex internal structure we must ask which *aspects* of the concept are or are not understood via metaphor.

112

We can now turn to the Grounding Hypothesis. This hypothesis addresses the question of how metaphorical understanding is possible at all. Generally, it states that metaphorical understanding is grounded in nonmetaphorical understanding. But, because of the complexity of metaphorical understanding, it must be stated more precisely than that.

The Grounding Hypothesis

— Many conventional concepts are semantically autonomous or have aspects that are semantically autonomous.
— Semantically autonomous concepts (or aspects of concepts) are grounded in the habitual and routine bodily and social patterns we experience, and in what we learn of the experience of others.
   Semantically autonomous concepts (or aspects of concepts) are not mind-free. They are not somehow given to us directly by the objective world. They are instead grounded in the patterns of experience that we routinely live.
— The source domain of a metaphor is characterized in terms of concepts (or aspects of concepts) that are semantically autonomous.
— In this sense, metaphorical understanding is grounded in semantically autonomous conceptual structure.

For the sake of further clarification, let us consider some examples. When we understand death as night, we are drawing on a semantically autonomous conventional understanding of the source domain, night. That understanding is grounded in what we experience night to be, namely, dark, cold, foreboding, and so on. And what we experience night to be depends upon both our sensory apparatus and what we have learned about night from our culture. Of course, a scientific understanding of night in terms of the rotation of the earth away from the sun is completely irrelevant here. It is only the commonplace experience of night as we ordinarily take it to be that matters.

Similarly, when we comprehend life as a journey, we are drawing upon a semantically autonomous conventional understanding of what a journey is: it has a starting point, endpoint, path, places we want to reach along the way, and, commonly, companions, difficulties, provisions, and so on. This semantically autonomous understanding of journeys is grounded in what we experience of journeys and in what we learn of journeys through our culture.

For the sake of the present discussion, it is important to bear in mind that the Grounding Hypothesis is about concepts, not about language. Moreover, it concerns only some concepts, or aspects of them—those that are semantically autonomous. Conventional concepts or aspects of concepts that are primarily grasped through metaphor (such as purpose, love, thought, time, and so on) are not semantically autonomous and so do not serve as the ultimate grounding for other metaphorical concepts.

Moreover, the Grounding Hypothesis concerns our experience rather than some objective, external, "mind-free" reality. It is important to bear all this in mind as we discuss the Literal Meaning Theory, which is about language and which does concern an objective, "mind-free" reality. The difference between the Grounding Hypothesis and the Literal Meaning Theory is all-important. We believe that the Grounding Hypothesis is correct and that the Literal Meaning Theory not only is incorrect but also leads to many other fallacies.

LITERAL MEANING

The Literal Meaning Theory is about language, not concepts. In particular, it is about ordinary, conventional language. The general thrust of the theory is to claim that *all* ordinary, conventional language (called "literal language") is semantically autonomous, that it forms the basis for metaphor, and that metaphor stands outside of it. But the theory is somewhat subtler than that and needs to be stated with more precision.

The Literal Meaning Theory

— If an expression of a language is (1) conventional and ordinary, then it is also (2) semantically autonomous and (3) capable of making reference to objective reality.

— Such a linguistic expression is called "literal."

— No metaphors are literal.

Objective reality is taken to have an existence independent of any human understanding; that is, it is taken to be "mind-free." Consequently, statements made in ordinary, conventional language are capable of being objectively true or false. The notion of "literal meaning" presupposes the truth of the Literal Meaning Theory, and *within that theory* the term "literal" is taken to apply to those expressions of a language that meet all of conditions 1, 2, and 3. Given this theory, all ordinary, conventional language is called "literal language" and is assumed to meet conditions 2 and 3.

The Literal Meaning Theory has certain immediate consequences. First, no ordinary conventional language can be metaphorical in any way. Second, all concepts expressed by ordinary conventional language must be semantically autonomous and hence not metaphorical. This is in accord with the common philosophical view that all concepts are reflections of objective reality, and hence cannot be metaphorical. What we will argue is that the Literal Meaning Theory, in terms of which the concept "literal" is defined, is incorrect on empirical grounds. Then we will show that the traditional concept of literal meaning is not appropriate for discussions of real language.

There are two empirically testable claims implicit in the characterization of the concept "literal meaning": the Autonomy Claim that all expressions meeting condition 1 also meet condition 2, and the Objectivist Claim that all expressions that meet condition 1 also meet condition 3. The very concept of literal meaning makes sense only if these two implicit claims are true. If either the Autonomy Claim or the Objectivist Claim is empirically incorrect, then the concept of literal meaning is not applicable to real natural language because the background conditions needed to make sense of the concept do not hold.

The evidence discussed in chapter one, together with the evidence discussed in the metaphor literature (see Bibliography), shows that both of these implicit claims are empirically false, and therefore that the Literal Meaning Theory is false. As a result, we maintain that the concept of "literal meaning" as it has traditionally been used is not appropriate to the discussion of real natural language. To see why, let us consider these two implicit claims, one by one.

The Autonomy Claim. The Autonomy Claim is that ordinary, conventional language is semantically autonomous and that therefore it is not metaphoric. But we have argued throughout this book that conventional language and our conventional conceptual system are fundamentally and ineradicably metaphoric. The argument that we have made again and again is that there are general mappings across conceptual domains that account for the understanding of both poetic and everyday conventional language. If the Autonomy Claim were true, this would be impossible.

For example, if the Autonomy Claim were true, then everything we have said about there being, say, a conventional LIFE IS A JOURNEY metaphor would be false. But to give up such metaphorical mappings would be to give up both true linguistic generalizations as well as explanations in two areas: explanations for use of the same words across conceptual domains and explanations for the use of the same inference patterns across conceptual domains.

First, without such a conceptual metaphor as LIFE IS A JOURNEY, there would be no conceptual unity to such ordinary conventional expressions as "making one's way in life," "giving one's life some direction," "getting somewhere with one's life," and so on. And there would be no explanation for the use of the same expressions like "making one's way," "direction," and "getting somewhere" in the domains of both traveling and living.

Second, without a LIFE IS A JOURNEY metaphor, there would be no explanation for how we can understand such poetic expressions as Frost's "Two roads diverged in a wood, and I— / I took the one less traveled by . . ." That is, there would be no way to explain either why we understand this passage to be about life or why we reason about it as we do.

Third, there would be no way to characterize the unity

between such poetic expressions and the corresponding everyday expressions.

The theory of conventional metaphor explains a number of phenomena: how everyday expressions are related by general principles; why the same expressions are used in different conceptual domains and why they mean what they do; how those general principles can explain the way that poetic metaphor is understood; and how those principles account for inferences both in ordinary everyday expressions and in the novel expressions used by poets. If the Autonomy Claim were true, no such explanations would be possible. Because those general principles and the explanations they afford seem to us to be fundamentally correct, we find more than sufficient reason to reject the Autonomy Claim.

The Objectivist Claim. The Objectivist Claim depends on a background assumption:

> "Objective reality" consists of states of affairs in the world independent of any human conceptualization or understanding. To be more precise, the world comes structured in a way that is objective—independent of any minds. The world as objectively structured includes objects, properties of those objects, relations holding among those objects, and categories of those objects, properties and relations.

The Objectivist Claim takes this for granted; the claim is:

> Conventional expressions in a language designate aspects of an objective, mind-free reality. Therefore, a statement must objectively be either true or false, depending on whether the objective world accords with the statement.

It is a consequence of the Objectivist Claim that all conventional expressions in a language are semantically autonomous and no expression can be understood, in whole or in part, by metaphor. On this view, there could be no such things as conceptual metaphors, which are mappings across conceptual domains, because such mappings could not exist in the objective, mind-free world. If expressions of a language are defined only in terms of a mind-free objective reality, then metaphors cannot enter into the characterization of the meanings of linguistic expressions, since metaphors are not mind-free.

The major fallacy behind the Objectivist Claim is that it does not recognize that truth and falsity are relative to conceptual frameworks. Thus, it fails to recognize that a statement can be meaningful only relative to its defining framework, and it can be true or false only relative to the way we understand reality given that framework. Since conceptual frameworks are products of the human mind, the structure of reality as it is reflected in human language is not objective in the technical sense, that is, not mind-free.

Many of our conceptual frameworks are metaphorical in nature. When we conceptualize life as a journey or birth as arrival, then our statements about life or birth can be true or false relative to those metaphorical conceptualizations. For example, it can be true of someone that he has no direction in life or that he has taken a slow, hard path or that he had a head start in life. But these things can be true only if one conceptualizes life via the LIFE IS A JOURNEY metaphor. Or if birth is conceptualized metaphorically as arrival here, then it is *false* that a newborn has just gone out of our life. It is *true* that the infant has just come into our life.

According to the Objectivist Claim, none of this makes any sense. Truth and falsity are absolutes and cannot be characterized relative to any metaphorical understanding. Moreover, the Objectivist Claim entails that, if we understand reality in terms of concepts within our conceptual system, then all such concepts can only be semantically autonomous and none are defined in terms of metaphor. Thus, the very idea that the concept of LIFE is understood metaphorically as a JOURNEY violates the Objectivist Claim, as does the idea that true or false statements might be relative to such an understanding.

Thus, if the arguments and analyses we have given so far in this book are correct, then the Autonomy and Objectivist Claims must both be false. If these are false, then the Literal Meaning Theory is false. And if the Literal Meaning Theory is false, the concept "literal meaning," which is defined relative to that theory, is not appropriate to the analysis of real natural language.

However, the term "literal" does exist and is not likely to disappear. We would like to suggest that it be defined so as to free it from the Literal Meaning Theory and give it a useful function. We suggest that the term "literal" be used as a handy, nontechnical term either for a source domain of a metaphor or to contrast with such terms as "ironic," "exaggerated," "understated," "arrived at by principles of conversation," and so on.

LITERAL MEANING VERSUS GROUNDING

It is important to see all the ways in which the Grounding Hypothesis differs from the Literal Meaning Theory.

First, the Grounding Hypothesis says that only *some* concepts are semantically autonomous. It is compatible with our view that *most* concepts are not semantically autonomous. This is very different from the Autonomy Claim of the Literal Meaning Theory, which says that *all* the concepts conventionally expressed by the words and phrases in a language are semantically autonomous.

Second, the Grounding Hypothesis is independent of the Objectivist Claim, which entails that the meanings of all concepts are characterized via reference to an objective, mind-free reality. We strongly deny that and claim rather that what semantically autonomous concepts there are are grounded in our patterns of bodily and social experience. The Grounding Hypothesis does not require that the semantically autonomous concepts be a direct mirror of a mind-free external reality, as the Literal Meaning Theory does.

Third, the Grounding Hypothesis is about *concepts*, not about *language*. The Grounding Hypothesis thus says nothing whatever about whether any *linguistic expressions* are semantically autonomous. On the Grounding Hypothesis, it could be the case that every word or phrase in a language is defined at least in part metaphorically, though semantically autonomous concepts would play a crucial role and would ground all conventionalized conceptual metaphors. We take this to be an open empirical question, to be determined by future study. The answer to this question has no bearing, one way or the other, on the theory of metaphor we have proposed. We have arrived at that theory on the basis of evidence, evidence concerning generalizations that govern the use of words and of inference patterns, and we feel that the theory is overwhelmingly supported by such evidence. Correspondingly, we feel that such evidence overwhelmingly disconfirms the Literal Meaning Theory.

SPINOFFS OF THE LITERAL MEANING THEORY

The Literal Meaning Theory has had a widespread effect and has led to a variety of other positions about metaphor, most of which arise quite often in the metaphor literature. Since these positions are consequences of the Literal Meaning Theory, we maintain that they too are false, for the same reasons. We will take these positions up one at a time.

The Paraphrase Position. According to the Literal Meaning Theory, a sentence can be meaningful only if it expresses a proposition that can be true or false, that is, that can characterize a state of affairs in "the objective, mind-free world." On this view, a metaphorical expression can be meaningful only if it can be paraphrased in language that is nonmetaphorical, that is, "literal language."

The Paraphrase Position fails to account for both the inferential and conceptualizing capacity of metaphor. Let us begin with the inferential capacity of metaphor. Consider the LIFE IS A JOURNEY metaphor. This way of conceptualizing life brings with it a complex structure of inferences which do not exist independent of the metaphor. Compare, for example, the difference in conceptualization between taking a given path in life and merely making a choice about one's life. When we understand making a choice as taking a path, there are immediate inferences that follow as a consequence of the metaphor: just as people on different paths are not together, so people making different choices are metaphorically not together; just as pursuing one path would require us to backtrack in order to take the other path, so proceeding along one path in life entails that if we want to take the other path we have to get back to the origin first; just as taking a path means facing what is coming up in the future, so making a choice is metaphorically facing what is coming up as a consequence of that choice.

None of this inferential work is immediately entailed merely by the nonmetaphoric concept of making a choice. Therefore, the metaphoric concept is not replaceable by the nonmetaphoric concept, and so a paraphrase eliminating the metaphor does not do the same job. Consider, for example, Frost's lines:

> Two roads diverged in a wood, and I—
> I took the one less traveled by,
> And that has made all the difference.

A paraphrase might say that there were two options to choose between, and that the speaker made the choice less frequently made. But this paraphrase fails to include all the inferences of the metaphor: that the speaker was making a choice to go forward to something he had not been to before, rather than backward to a previous state; that the speaker parted company upon making this choice with those who made other choices; that the speaker came upon this moment of decision by being confronted with alternative but mutually exclusive choices; and so on.

The case is exactly the same with the metaphor that BIRTH IS ARRIVAL HERE. We can think nonmetaphorically of life in this sense: first we are not alive, then we are born, then we live for a while, and then we are dead. But these nonmetaphoric concepts cannot replace BIRTH IS ARRIVAL HERE. For example, these concepts do not contain the metaphoric notion that being alive, which is a state, is also, metaphorically, a location; that a change of state is a change of location and therefore an arrival at that new location. The nonmetaphoric conceptualization of life does not capture the concept that being alive is metaphorically *here*. Why should being alive not be metaphorically *there*? In the metaphoric conceptualization, the image-schema of a bounded space is mapped onto the domain of life, making life here, and what is exterior to life not here. This spatial understanding comes only with the metaphor. Consequently, no nonmetaphoric paraphrase can replace a poetic metaphor about birth as arrival here. We cannot accurately paraphrase Shakespeare's "Thou must have patience; we came crying hither," as "You must be patient. When we were first born, we cried."

Of course, we might attempt to *describe*, as opposed to *paraphrase*, a conceptual metaphor, which we have been doing throughout this book. We might even attempt to do a partial description without using conventional metaphoric language, which would be hard. But in no case would our supposedly nonmetaphoric description replace the metaphor.

This is especially clear in the case of poems whose point is to present an image-mapping, as, for example, in the following poem translated from the Sanskrit:

> Earth with new grass
> and color of young ladybugs
> shines
> parrot
> woman lying under green blanket
> after red sun shower
> (*The Peacock's Egg*, p. 59)

The poem presents two image-metaphors. First the image of the green grass and reddish ladybugs is mapped on the parrot's green plumage with reddish spots, and then it is further mapped onto the image of a woman under a green blanket sprinkled with raindrops reflecting the red of the sun. Such image-metaphors cannot be eliminated in favor of a paraphrase.

The Decoding Position. This is a special case of the Paraphrase Position. It claims that a metaphor is merely part of a code to be broken, in order to reveal the nonmetaphoric concepts that the author is trying indirectly to express. The decoding mistake underlies the common misleading phrase that "x is a metaphor for y," as when we say "in this line, wind is a metaphor for change." The mistaken conception underlying these statements is that the source domain merely gives a set of words that are a kind of symbolic code for referring to concepts in the target domain that are understood independently of the metaphor.

The Similarity Position. According to the Literal Meaning Theory, all of our concepts are "literal"; that is, they do not make use of any metaphoric *mappings* across conceptual domains or any *understanding* of one concept in terms of another. This leads to the view that noticing a metaphoric connection between two concepts is no more than noticing that the two concepts share some "literal," nonmetaphoric properties. Metaphor, on this view, is merely a spotlight, bringing to our attention the details of the similarity between two nonmetaphoric concepts but having no effect on the structure of those concepts or on the understanding of them. On this view, the sole conceptual power metaphor might have is to highlight similarities that are already there. We have shown that, on the contrary, metaphor can provide structure and attributes not inherent in the target domain, as, for example, when dying is understood as departure to a final destination or death is understood as a reaper. The phenomenon of death is not objectively similar to a reaper.

To deny the traditional Similarity Position is not to deny that similarity *of some kind* is involved in metaphor, even if it not a similarity of objective, nonmetaphoric properties. The hypothesis that metaphors preserve image-schema structure has as a conclusion that when a target domain is understood metaphorically, it will share some image-schematic structure with the source domain, structure that may have been in part introduced by the metaphor. In short, on our view, metaphor always results in a similarity of image-schema structure between the source and target domains. This is by no means the traditional Similarity Position. But it is a theory in which similarity of a limited special kind does play a role.

The Reason-versus-Imagination Position. The Literal Meaning Theory entails another position, the assumption that reason and imagination are mutually exclusive. Reason is taken to be the rational linking up of concepts, which are nonmetaphoric, so as to lead from true premises to true conclusions. Thus, there is nothing metaphoric about reason, neither its operations nor the concepts it operates on. Metaphoric reasoning, on this view, cannot exist. Since metaphor is excluded from the domain of reason, it is left for the domain of imagination, which is assumed to be fanciful and irrational.

This view is, as we have seen repeatedly, erroneous. Many of our inferences are metaphoric: we often reason *metaphorically*, as when we conclude that if John has lost direction, then he has not yet reached his goal. Our reasoning that time changes things is metaphoric and deeply indispensable to how we think about events in the physical, social, and biological worlds. Indeed, so much of our reason is metaphoric that if we view metaphor as part of the faculty of the imagination, then reason is mostly if not entirely imaginative in character.

The Naming Position. The Literal Meaning Theory comes with a notion of the "proper" use of words: in their "proper" use, words designate literal concepts, concepts that are autonomous and can characterize states of affairs in the real world. The Naming Position says that a metaphor is the use of a word to mean something it doesn't "properly" mean. Metaphor would, thus, be no more than a use of words, and an improper one at that. This position has the false consequence that metaphor has no conceptual role; in other words, it cannot be used in reasoning, conceptualizing, and understanding.

The Deviance Position. According to the Literal Meaning Theory, all concepts and conventional language are nonmetaphoric, and we make metaphors only by deviating from normal conventional usage. To assume the Deviance Position is to see all metaphorical language as deviant. But as we have seen, our ordinary everyday language is ineradicably metaphoric. We speak constantly of people passing away, being drawn to someone emotionally, feeling up or down, and so on. Conventional metaphorical thought and language are normal, not deviant.

The Fallback Position. The Literal Meaning Theory assumes that the normal use of language is nonmetaphoric, and therefore we look *first* for the literal meaning of a sentence (a composition of the literal meanings of the words in that sentence), and seek a metaphorical meaning (that is, a paraphrase) only as a fallback, if we are not content with the primary literal meaning. But, as we have seen, our concepts in certain domains are often *primarily metaphorical*, as when we understand death as departure, loss, sleep, and so on.

The Pragmatics Position. Under the Literal Meaning Theory, the use of metaphor lies outside of normal, conventional language that can be true or false. This places it outside of the traditional characterization of "semantics." Though we would use the term to refer to meaning of any kind, metaphorical or not, "semantics" has a traditional sense taken from philosophical logic that includes under its purview only conventional language that can be true or false. Other aspects of interpretation are assumed to arise from language use and are lumped under the rubric of "pragmatics." Metaphor is traditionally assumed to fall under the pragmatic rubric. On this account, no conventional metaphor is considered metaphor at all; only novel metaphorical expressions count.

The Pragmatics Position, as usually articulated, incorporates many of the positions cited above: the Literal Meaning Theory, the Deviance Position, the Paraphrase Position, and the Fallback Position. It assumes (1) that metaphorical expressions are not literal; (2) that they are deviant; (3) that the meanings of metaphorical expressions are paraphrases, that is, they are meanings of other literal expressions; and (4) that one first tries to understand them literally and resorts to a metaphorical reading only if a literal reading is impossible. Given all these assumptions, the Pragmatics Position claims that the meaning of a metaphor is arrived at by taking its (semantically ill-formed) literal meaning and applying to it pragmatic principles of conversation that yield the meaning of the metaphor as a result.

The Pragmatics Position has all of the flaws of the Literal Meaning, Deviance, Paraphrase, and Fallback Positions.

But the central mistake is in the characterization of "semantics" in terms of the Literal Meaning Theory, and the use of the Literal Meaning Theory in drawing the traditional semantics-pragmatics distinction. Once that distinction is drawn, metaphor *must* be a matter of pragmatics, that is, purely a matter of language use rather than conceptual structure. Our reply is that the traditional semantics-pragmatics distinction that lies behind this theory is false, because the Literal Meaning Theory is false.

Incidentally, our claim that metaphor is not purely a matter of pragmatics does not mean that principles of conversation never enter into metaphorical understanding. On the contrary, we will show in chapter four that such principles often combine with conceptual metaphors in the understanding of poetry.

The No Concepts Position. This position arises from the popular philosophical theory that views the meaning of expressions in a language as independent of human cognition. "Semantics," on this view, is a matter of the relation of words to the world. Expressions of a language are seen as getting their meaning by directly designating aspects of objective reality, without the intervention of a human conceptual system. Because language, on this view, is not based on any conceptual system, there is no distinction to be drawn between the meanings of words and the meanings of concepts.

On this position, the Literal Meaning Theory must be true. Conventional expressions of a language must be semantically autonomous since they get their meaning only by designating aspects of objective reality. Consequently, sentences must be either objectively true (if they accord with reality) or false (if they do not).

Since meaning resides only in the relation between words and the world, independent of human cognition and conceptual systems, several things follow. (1) Conventional expressions cannot be metaphorical; there can be no such thing as conventional metaphor. (2) Metaphor cannot be a matter of mappings in the human conceptual system, since there is no conceptual system on which language is based. (3) The meaning of a metaphorical expression can only be

126

the literal meaning of the expression, since that is the only kind of meaning there is. There is no such thing as metaphorical meaning. On the whole, the metaphors are trivially false, though they may on occasion be trivially true. (4) Since there are no concepts, language is neither a matter of representation (of the external world in terms of mental concepts) nor a means of expression for such concepts. (5) Metaphors are properly seen as being outside of conventional language. For a metaphor to have a nontrivial meaning is for it to enter the literal language and cease to be a metaphor (thus, to become a "dead metaphor").

Since the No Concepts Position includes the Literal Meaning Theory and the Deviance Position, it has all the drawbacks that those positions have. In addition, it has the drawback of incorporating the Dead Metaphor Theory, which we discuss in detail below.

Sources of the Literal Meaning Theory. Two common oversights are behind the popularity of the Literal Meaning Theory. Both have to do with the Autonomy Claim. Conventional language and thought have two aspects that are often overlooked: conventional language works by general principles and it has an automatic, unconscious character. Because the general principles governing metaphor exist at the conceptual level, they are commonly overlooked by approaches to the study of language that ignore cognition. If one fails to look for such general principles, then one will overlook all of the conventional metaphors we have discussed, and it may appear as though conventional language and thought have no metaphor.

A second common oversight is to miss the automatic and unconscious character of conventional thought and language. *The conventional aspects of language are the ones that are most alive,* in the sense that they are embodied in our minds, are constantly used, and affect the way we think and talk every day. The fact that linguistic mechanisms are conventional means that they are fixed, that they are not made up anew each time we use them; conventional metaphorical expressions that are part of a live system are also fixed. Because they are fixed, they are sometimes mistaken for dead.

If one makes this mistake, then one might think that conventional language has no live metaphors.

These two oversights have contributed to the popularity of the Literal Meaning Theory and are therefore worth discussing in some detail.

THE FAILURE-TO-GENERALIZE METHODOLOGY

As we have seen, the generalizations about metaphor can be stated in terms of systematic mappings at the conceptual level. Such mappings have great explanatory power. Not surprisingly, if one fails to seek such general conceptual mappings, one will not find them. There are two common sources of such failings. The first, which we will call the Case-by-case Methodology, consists simply in ignoring the existence of the systematic principles relating individual metaphorical expressions. Consequently, one analyzes each individual metaphorical expression as if it were unrelated to any other.

The second, which we will call the Source-domain-only Error, is to fail to look at the mapping from source to target, and instead to consider only the source domain. For example, consider "old flame" and "fiery youth." In both, the source domain is fire, and so it is an easy mistake to lump them together as "fire metaphors" and to assume that they work by the same process. But in fact, "old flame" is based on the LOVE IS FIRE metaphor, and "fiery youth" on the LIFE IS FIRE metaphor. While source domain is the same, the target domains, and therefore the mappings, are different. The moral is that a metaphor is a systematic conceptual mapping involving *two* domains; it is not just an expression from a source domain.

THE DEAD METAPHOR THEORY

One reason that some theorists have not come to grips with the fact that ordinary everyday language is inescapably metaphoric is that they hold the belief that all metaphors that are conventional are "dead"—they are not metaphors any longer, though they once might have been. This position, which fails to distinguish between conventional metaphors, which are part of our live conceptual system, and historical metaphors that have long since died out, constitutes the Dead Metaphor Theory.

Suppose we encounter a word like "gone" in an expression like "He's almost gone," used of a dying person. The Dead Metaphor Theory would claim that "gone" isn't really metaphoric now, though it once may have been. "Gone" has simply come to have "dead" as one of its meanings.

The mistake derives from a basic confusion: it assumes that those things in our cognition that are most alive and most active are those that are conscious. On the contrary, those that are most alive and most deeply entrenched, efficient, and powerful are those that are so automatic as to be unconscious and effortless. Our understanding of life as a journey is active and widespread, but effortless and unconscious. Part of the evidence that conventional metaphors exist as live aspects of cognition is their occurrence in novel poetic creations, like those we have discussed throughout this book. If those metaphors did not exist at all in our conceptual systems, then we could not understand novel, unconventional poetic language that makes use of them.

What makes the Dead Metaphor Theory believable to some people is that there are indeed expressions that were once metaphoric and now no longer are. The word "pedigree," for example, came from the Old French "pied de grue," which meant "foot of a crane." It was based on an image-metaphor which mapped the shape of a crane's foot onto a family tree diagram. That image-metaphor no longer exists at the conceptual level, and at the linguistic level we do not use "pedigree" to mean "crane's foot." This is a truly dead metaphor—at both levels.

Other metaphors can be dead at just one level. Compare, for example, the words "comprehend" and "grasp." Today, there is a live conceptual metaphor in which UNDERSTAND-ING IS GRASPING, and we use the word "grasp" to mean understand. The same conceptual metaphor existed in Latin, where the word "comprehendere" meant basically to grasp, and, by metaphoric extension, to understand. Now we use it only in its metaphoric sense; its former central sense is dead for us. But the old conceptual metaphor is still alive, though it is not used in this word.

Determining whether a given metaphor is dead or just unconsciously conventional is not always an easy matter. It might require, among other things, a search for its systematic manifestation in the language as a whole and in our everyday reasoning patterns. However, there are plenty of clear cases of basic conventional metaphors that are alive,— hundreds of them—certainly enough to show that what is conventional and fixed need not be dead.

At this point we can see why the Dead Metaphor Theory has been so popular. It is a consequence of the Literal Meaning Theory. On the Literal Meaning Theory, ordinary conventional expressions cannot be metaphoric. Thus, if an expression looks like a metaphor but is part of the ordinary conventional language, then it cannot really be a metaphor, since ordinary conventional language is all literal. But that does not rule out the possibility that it once was a metaphor and became literal. On the Literal Meaning Theory, this is the only possible explanation why something that is literal can look like a metaphor. If one accepts the Literal Meaning Theory, one must accept the Dead Metaphor Theory as a consequence.

In recent years, historical study of how words change their meanings has shown that the Dead Metaphor Theory is false. Sweetser[4] has shown that the same kinds of meaning change recur over and over through the history of the Indo-European languages. For example, words meaning "see" regularly acquire the meaning of "know" at widely scattered times and places. The theory of conceptual metaphor that we have advanced explains why this is so: there is a widespread and ancient conceptual metaphor that KNOWING IS SEEING. ("Wit" and "vision" have the same Indo-European root.) Because that metaphor exists in the conceptual systems of Indo-Eurpoean speakers, the conceptual mapping between seeing and knowing defines what Sweetser calls a "pathway" for semantic change, so that as new words for seeing develop they eventually extend their

----

[4] See Eve Sweetser, *From Etymology to Pragmatics: The Mind-as-Body Metaphor in Semantic Structure and Semantic Change* (Cambridge: Cambridge University Press, in press).

meanings to knowing. Without such a theory of conceptual metaphor, there is no reason why the same changes should occur over and over.

The various positions on metaphor that we have considered so far are really aspects of one multifaceted theory—the Literal Meaning Theory. It begins with two basic misunderstandings of the nature of conventional language and thought and then extends them methodically to produce additional mistaken views. Almost all of what we take to be incorrect accounts of metaphor flow from this one fundamental mistake. To our knowledge, there is only one basic mistake in the various theories of metaphor that is independent of the Literal Meaning Theory. Let us turn to it now.

The Interaction Theory

The Interaction Theory arises from a correct observation. Suppose a source and target domain are linked by a conventional metaphor. Speaking about the source domain alone may bring to mind the target domain. For example, an extensive discussion of a journey may lead one to reflect on the course of one's life. Given the theory we have advanced, this is not at all surprising: when metaphoric connections are conventionalized, they may become activated by discussion of the source domain alone. Discussing a particular journey may activate the LIFE IS A JOURNEY metaphor, resulting in an effortless and virtually unconscious mapping of aspects of the journey under discussion onto aspects of one's life.

Unfortunately, this very real phenomenon has been analyzed incorrectly as follows: the target domain is described as "suffusing" the source domain, and it is claimed that the metaphor is bidirectional—from target to source as well as from source to target. Indeed, according to this theory, there is no source or target. There is only a connection across domains, with one concept seen through the filter of the other. Here's what is wrong with such an analysis.

When we understand that life is a journey we structure life in terms of a journey, and map onto the domain of life the inferential structure associated with journeys. But we do not map onto the domain of journeys the inferential structure associated with the domain of life. For example, we do not understand thereby that journeys have waking and sleeping parts, as lives do. We do not infer that, just as we can lead only one life, so a traveler can take only one journey. We map one way only, from the source domain of journey onto the target domain of life.

The Interaction Theory assumes that in saying that life is a journey, we are merely comparing the two domains in both directions and picking out the similarities. If this were true, then our language should go both ways as well. We should speak of journeys conventionally in the language of life, perhaps calling embarcations "births" and departures "deaths." When someone takes a trip, one would expect to be able to say something like "He was born," and mean, conventionally, "He started his trip." Since metaphorical mapping is always partial, we would not necessarily expect all of these, but we would expect some.

Of course, two different metaphors might share two domains but differ in which is source and which is target, and also differ in what gets mapped onto what. We can have cases like PEOPLE ARE MACHINES, as in

> At the violet hour, when the eyes and back
> Turn upward from the desk, when the human engine
>   waits
> Like a taxi throbbing waiting
> (Eliot, *The Waste Land*)

and also the different metaphor MACHINES ARE PEOPLE, as when we say, "The computer is punishing me by wiping out my buffer." But these are two different metaphors, because the mappings go in opposite directions, *and different things get mapped*. In MACHINES ARE PEOPLE, the will and desire of a person are attributed to machines, but in the PEOPLE ARE MACHINES metaphor, there is no mention of will and desire. What is mapped instead is the fact that machines have parts that function in certain ways, such as idling steadily or accelerating, that they break down and may need to be fixed, and so on.

Of course, a poet might use these two separate and apparently converse metaphors adjacently, and bring them into play with each other. We can easily imagine, for example, a poem about the relationship between a human and his computer, in which the human is metaphorically presented in terms of his machine, and the machine is metaphorically presented in terms of its human user. But this would be a use of two different conceptual metaphors performing different mappings.

In short, there is no evidence for the Interaction Theory. The phenomenon that gave rise to it can be accounted for in terms of the theory we have advanced. The predictions made by the claim of bidirectionality are not borne out, since neither the logic nor the language of the target domain is mapped onto the source domain. And finally, where there are domains A and B with mappings both from A to B and from B to A, they turn out to be different mappings rather than a single bidirectional mapping.

The Linguistic-expressions-only Position. It is extremely common to see metaphor as a matter of linguistic expressions alone and not of conceptual structure. This is the assumption behind the grammar-school distinction between metaphor and simile: given that A is not literally B, a metaphor is a statement of the form "A is B," while a simile is a statement of the form "A is like B."

This attempt to define metaphor in terms of syntactic form misses entirely what metaphor is about: the understanding of one concept in terms of another. Statements of both forms can employ conceptual metaphor. The kind called a simile simply makes a weaker claim. To say "An atom is like a small solar system" uses essentially the same conceptual metaphor as "An atom is a small solar system," only the simile hedges its bets—it makes a weaker claim. But in both cases, one concept (atom) is being understood in terms of another (solar system). On the whole, the syntactic form of an utterance has little, if anything, to do with whether metaphor is involved in comprehending it.

The It's All Metaphor Position. We began this chapter by discussing this position, and so it is fitting to close with it. Actually, there are two importantly different positions to be isolated: a strong position and a weak position. The strong position is:

> Every aspect of every concept is completely understood via metaphor.

From this it follows that:

Every linguistic expression is completely understood via metaphor.

The weak position is:

> Every linguistic expression expresses a concept that is, at least in some aspect, understood via metaphor.

The weak position is the less interesting of the two, and it may be correct. For example, we saw above that in understanding dogs as loyal and lions as courageous, we are metaphorically attributing to them human characteristics and thus comprehending them, *in some small part*, in metaphorical terms. The bulk of our understanding of these concepts is, of course, not metaphorical at all. In addition, we understand states as locations (more precisely, bounded regions) in space and changes as movements into or out of such regions. There are a great many concepts of state and change. Take *hot* and *heat up*. It is perfectly sensible to say that *hot*, in that it is a state, is understood metaphorically as a region in space. Of course, it is only one aspect of *hot* that is so understood—the aspect that it shares with *cold*, *tall*, and all other stative predicates. To say that this aspect of *hot* is metaphorical is consistent with the view that the bulk of the concept is not metaphorically understood.

The weak position is thus rather tame, hardly in the spirit of the strong It's All Metaphor Position, since it is consistent with the claim that most aspects of most concepts are not metaphorical. What *is* particularly interesting about the weak position is that it shows how important it is to distinguish concepts from expressions in a language when discussing metaphor. On the weak position, it could be true that a very large number of *concepts* are not understood via metaphor, and at the same time it could also be true that *every linguistic expression* of every language is understood via metaphor, at least in part. The reason is that an expression of a language can designate a complex concept, which can be metaphorical in some aspects but not others. If the distinction between concepts and linguistic expressions is not made—if only expressions in a language are considered—then the weak and the strong positions cannot be distinguished.

We take no stand on the weak position. On empirical grounds, all that we are in a position to maintain on this issue is that at least some aspects of a great many concepts and conventional linguistic expressions are metaphorical.

The strong position is another matter. It seems false. Metaphors allow us to understand one domain of experience in terms of another. To serve this function, there must be some grounding, some concepts that are not completely understood via metaphor to serve as source domains. There seems to be no shortage of such concepts. A brief survey of the source domains mentioned in this book yields many concepts that are at least partly, if not totally, understood on their own terms: plants, departures, fire, sleep, locations, seeing, and so on.

Of course, we do not mean that it is not possible to construct metaphors in which these concepts are the targets. Consider, for example, Emerson's lines, "Though her parting dims the day, / Stealing grace from all alive." Here, a certain departure is a target domain, and it is understood both in terms of a diminishing of the intensity of light and in terms of the actions of a thief. In saying that these concepts like plants and departures are at least partly understood on their own terms and not metaphorically, we mean exactly that we have no evidence that any of them is conventionally, automatically, and unconsciously understood in terms of some completely different conceptual domain. We do not, for example, automatically understand *departure* in terms of *sunset*; we do not conventionally understand *absence* in terms of *winter*—even though Shakespeare can write, "How like a winter hath my absence been."

CONCLUSION

Metaphor has been studied and theorized about for over two millenia. Unfortunately, most scholars have been led astray by the Literal Meaning Theory and related doctrines. And they have not, for the most part, looked for generalizations at the conceptual level that govern many different linguistic expressions of metaphorical ideas. These are the two major sources of failure in the traditional theories.

A guide to further reading. We have done our best to survey the principal traditional theories of metaphor and where our views differ from them. Our survey differs from most other such surveys in two respects: First, we have not tried to say who claims what, to associate particular authors with positions. Our main interest has been in simply stating what the positions are. Second, we have tried to make the background assumptions of these positions clear. For example, no author comes out and states that he believes the Literal Meaning Theory; it is just taken for granted. No one overtly states the Autonomy Claim. It is part of the background. But in order to provide evidence against them, one must make the implicit claims explicit.

For those readers who are interested in following up on traditional theories, we include a section called "More on Traditional Views" in the bibliography.

Metaphor Research as an Empirical Enterprise

On various traditional views, metaphor is a matter of unusual language, typically novel and poetic language, that strikes us as deviant, imaginative, and fanciful. We and other researchers have argued instead that metaphor is a conceptual matter, often unconscious, and that conceptual metaphors underlie everyday language as well as poetic language. We have arrived at these claims empirically, by studying many cases of both ordinary and poetic language and showing general principles underlying them. The claims we put forward are open to empirical corroboration or invalidation. Consider, for example, our claim in the analysis of EVENTS ARE ACTIONS that personifications arising from that metaphor must meet certain requirements before speakers of English will regard them as natural—for instance, the requirements that event structure and causal structure must be preserved by the metaphor. It is open to any researcher anywhere to demonstrate that we are wrong by coming up with a counterexample, namely, a personification that arises from that metaphor but that does not meet the requirements and that is still generally regarded as unexceptionable.

The empirical nature of the enterprise of analyzing metaphor is sometimes misunderstood. Sometimes, researchers have viewed metaphor not as a matter for empirical investigation but rather as a purely definitional matter. Such a view might lead to the criticism that in this book all we have done is to redefine metaphor: whereas metaphor is traditionally defined as a species of innovative language, we, so the claim would go, have simply redefined it as a species of conceptual mapping. We think that such a criticism reflects a profound misunderstanding of the enterprise of metaphor research, and we would like to dispel that misunderstanding.

There is, of course, a grain of truth behind the criticism: the term *metaphor* has traditionally been used to refer to a class of linguistic expressions of the sort commonly found in poetry. This book is filled with such examples. It is an empirical question as to whether each such poetic metaphor is completely unique and fully original, or whether there are general principles that lie behind individual metaphorical expressions.

For instance, we saw above that there was a metaphorical conception of a lifetime as a day in various poetic expressions, such as "In me thou seest the twilight of such day / As after darkness fadeth in the west," "Do not go gentle into that good night," "Alice . . . / Declines upon her lost and twilight age," and "but when our brief light goes out / there's one perpetual night to be slept through." It is an empirical observation that we understand all these expressions in terms of a single conceptual metaphor, namely, A LIFETIME IS A DAY. All these poetic expressions use different words. If a metaphor were no more than a linguistic expression, we could not say that these expressions are all instances of *the same metaphor;* they would simply be different expressions with nothing in common. Indeed, if a metaphor were no more than a linguistic expression, we could not speak at all of a *metaphorical conception* of a lifetime as a day, since there could be no such thing as a metaphorical conception.

It is a matter not of definitions but rather of theoretical *arguments*, supported by evidence and open to empirical corroboration or invalidation by other such evidence, that such general metaphors as A LIFETIME IS A DAY exist, that they are conceptual, not linguistic, in nature, and that they have the form of structural mappings across conceptual domains. It is only through hypothesizing conceptual mappings of this sort that we can reveal the general conceptual metaphors at work in particular poems.

We have used the term *metaphor* to refer to such conceptual mappings because they are what is responsible for the phenomenon traditionally called metaphor. It is the conceptual work that lies behind the language that makes metaphor what it is. Metaphorical language is not something special. It is the language that conventionally expresses the source-domain concept of a conceptual metaphor. Thus, in the lines above, "twilight" conventionally denotes twilight and "night" conventionally denotes night. It is the conceptual metaphor A LIFETIME IS A DAY that maps twilight onto old age and night onto death. The metaphorical work is being done at the conceptual level. For this reason we have used the term *metaphor* to characterize the conceptual mapping that does that work.

Finally, it is also a theoretical argument, based on empirical evidence, not a matter of definition, that conceptual metaphor lies behind much of ordinary everyday language. Conventional metaphorical language is simply a consequence of the existence of conventional metaphorical thought.

It is true that we are using the word "metaphor" in a nontraditional way. The reason we use the word this way is that we want the word to reflect our claims about the nature of all those poetic expressions that have traditionally been called metaphors. To accept the traditional use of the term would be to accept the traditional theories that guided that use of the term. As our understanding of the nature of metaphor changes, so the use of the term must change to accommodate what we have learned.

In the next chapter we will explore a major consequence of the conceptual nature of metaphor. So far, we have discussed metaphorical understanding expression by expression within a poem. But given a reading of a poem that makes use of the metaphorical understanding of the expressions in the poem one by one, it is often possible to derive a further, second-order metaphorical reading of the poem as a whole. Such global readings are based not on any particular expressions but rather on the overall meaning of the first-order reading. Second-order metaphorical readings, being free of particular linguistic expressions, make manifest the conceptual nature of metaphor. If metaphor were only a matter of words, such global second-order readings would not be possible.

THREE

The Metaphoric Structure
of a Single Poem

The Jasmine Lightness of the Moon

To a Solitary Disciple
Rather notice, mon cher,
that the moon is
tilted above
the point of the steeple
than that its color
is shell-pink.

Rather observe
that it is early morning
than that the sky
is smooth
as a turquoise.

Rather grasp
how the dark
converging lines
of the steeple
meet at the pinnacle—
perceive how
its little ornament
tries to stop them—

See how it fails!
See how the converging lines
of the hexagonal spire
escape upward—
receding, dividing!
—sepals
that guard and contain
the flower!

Observe
how motionless

140

the eaten moon
lies in the protecting lines.
It is true:
in the light colors
of morning
brown-stone and slate
shine orange and dark blue.

But observe
the oppressive weight
of the squat edifice!
Observe
the jasmine lightness
of the moon.
(William Carlos Williams)

Now that we have sketched the lines of a theory of poetic metaphor, it is time to look not at metaphors one by one but at the way a range of different conceptual metaphors can be combined to yield subtle and complex effects in a single reading of a single poem.

This poem, as we shall see, can be read as being metaphoric on two levels. First, it discusses how to look at a scene. In doing so, it makes considerable use of metaphor. Second, the poem as a whole can be given a metaphorical interpretation, in which the disciple to whom the poem is addressed is told how to understand the nature of religion in terms of the scene presented to him. First we will discuss the use of metaphor in the author's instructions for how to look at the scene. This will then lead us to a discussion of a metaphoric understanding of the poem as a whole.

At first glance, this poem may not seem especially laden with metaphor. There are some obvious cases—the eaten moon, the jasmine lightness, the lines as sepals of a flower. But, as we look closely, metaphors underlying our understanding of even the simplest lines appear. We need to look closely because some of them are such basic conceptual metaphors that we use them unconsciously and automatically, without effort, as part of our ordinary language.

Consider "the sky / is smooth / as a turquoise." How can something we see but not touch be smooth? How does smoothness apply to vision? There is a basic metaphor that

SEEING IS TOUCHING, where the eyes are understood as limbs that reach out and perceive what they touch, as in "Her eyes picked out every detail of the pattern," "He couldn't take his eyes off of her," "He ran his eyes over the page," "Their eyes met," and "His eyes traced the outline of the steeple." When we run our fingers across something smooth like a turquoise, nothing interrupts the continuous motion. Similarly, when we scan a perfectly empty, clear blue sky, there is nothing to stop our gaze, no clouds, no birds, no variation in visual texture. The metaphor of seeing-as-touching maps the uninterrupted tactile texture of the smooth stone onto the uninterrupted visual texture of the empty sky. The seeing as touching metaphor is thus a bridge that allows us to relate the tactile texture of the turquoise to the visual texture of the sky, automatically, without effort or notice. The same line also triggers an image-metaphor, mapping the blue of the turquoise onto the blue of the sky, without the bridge of SEEING IS TOUCHING. Two things are remarkable about this case. First, the same line triggers two different metaphors. Secondly, although both metaphors involve sensory mappings, they work differently: the color mapping is direct, while the texture mapping requires the intermediary SEEING IS TOUCHING metaphor.

Another line that might not at first be taken as metaphoric is "how the dark / converging lines / of the steeple / meet at the pinnacle—." It is common to speak of lines "converging" or "meeting," as if they were moving. We say that "the road runs on for a bit and then splits," "the path stretches along the shore of the lake," "the fence dips and rises in parallel with the terrain." Such language is based on a common way of understanding static shapes metaphorically in terms of a motion tracing that shape. For example, in "the roof slopes down," the roof isn't doing anything, but we understand its shape—that of a slope—in terms of a downward "sloping" motion. The metaphor here is that FORM IS MOTION, in which a form is understood in terms of the motion tracing the form.

This metaphor transforms a static schema into a dynamic one: a static form is understood as a dynamic motion. It is, of course, a metaphor that is grounded in experience, as when we trace a design on paper which results in a design being there. The words "converging" and "meet" in "the dark / converging lines / of the steeple / meet" make use of this metaphor. What makes a steeple seem to "point upward" is that its lines appear to move in an upward direction, "meeting" at the point. When an object moves, of course, it has momentum and can exert a force on anything in its path. Each line is in metaphorical motion. The motions converge at the apex of the steeple, and in the metaphor, their combined force is exerted on the ornament at the apex.

There are two metaphorical events here. First, the linear forces converge on the ornament. Second, the ornament remains unmoved. At this point, a second metaphor comes into play, the metaphor of EVENTS ARE ACTIONS. Both metaphorical events are thereby understood as actions. The lines are metaphorically in motion, and therefore are agents trying to escape, and the ornament's stasis is metaphorically an event of staying put, and therefore the ornament is an agent trying to stop this motion: "Perceive how / its little ornament / tries to stop them— / See how it fails! / See how the converging lines / of the hexagonal spire / escape upward."

The use of FORM IS MOTION to describe the lines converging and meeting is fully conventional. It is the normal way to think and talk about such a geometric figure. The existence of the form-as-motion metaphor makes the poet's extension of it seem natural. the image of the lines escaping makes sense only relative to their moving in the first place.

Until the phrase "tries to stop them," we are instructed to see things only as we might normally see them. Correspondingly, conventional metaphors are used only where we would normally use them, as in expressions like "converge" and "meet." It is at this point that the poet instructs the disciple to see something he would not normally see: the lines not merely moving, but trying to escape, the ornament trying to stop them, and the lines succeeding. And he does this by extending the use of conventional metaphor.

There are two extensions here: an extension of the FORM

IS MOTION metaphor and an extension of the EVENTS ARE ACTIONS metaphor. The events-as-actions metaphor is used conventionally in expressions such as "The boulder resisted all attempts to move it." Since motions are events and events can be seens as actions, the form-as-motion and events-as-actions metaphors can combine to describe static scenes as agentive motions, as in "the road runs up into the hills." At this point in the poem, EVENTS ARE ACTIONS is extended from such conventional ways of thinking about scenes to a new way: seeing the lines as trying to escape and the ornament as trying to stop them. Similarly, FORM IS MOTION is also conventionalized in English, as in such everyday expressions as "The mountain rises to an altitude of seven thousand feet," "The road dips just ahead," "The trees along the coast tilt landward," "The new freeway encircles the entire metropolitan area," and so on. It also underlies such poetic examples as Macbeth's "What, will the line stretch out to the crack of doom?" (4.1). FORM IS MOTION is extended at the same point in the poem as is EVENTS ARE ACTIONS, when the lines, instead of stopping where they meet, keep going and then "recede" and "divide." In this way, extended uses of everyday metaphors are employed to provide an extended vision of an everyday scene.

The new image we construct is an extension of our normal mode of understanding the static lines as being in motion. The conventional image thus gives rise to the novel image. When we understand that the ornament fails, it entails that the lines escape, continuing upward in their linear course to flank the moon, holding it in place, guarding it. The conventional metaphors of form as motion and events as actions make this extended image possible.

In addition to using conventional metaphors and extensions of them, the poem makes use of novel metaphors, especially image-metaphors. In the most striking of these, the lines flanking the moon become "—sepals / that guard and contain / the flower." The image of the flower is mapped onto the image of the moon, with the sepals—the outer green cover that contained the bud and that holds the petals to the stem—mapped onto the lines that have escaped from the steeple.

This image-metaphor results in a conceptual transformation: the rectilinear, static, inanimate, formally arranged lines of the hexagonal spire have become the curved, fluid, living, naturally soft form of the sepal. The abstract, general, platonic figure of a hexagon has become a concrete, particular part of a flower. The sepal is benign; it guards and protects the petals. Just so, the lines from the steeple guard and protect the moon. "Observe / how motionless / the eaten moon / lies in the protecting lines." Here there is another image-metaphor: the moon is "eaten." The shape of the moon is the shape of something round with a bite taken out. The shape thus, by metonymy, suggests the bite: the form implies the action. Both the resulting form and the action are part of the image-metaphor.

Just as there was an image-mapping of the hexagonal shape of the steeple onto the natural shape of a sepal, so there is an image-metaphor that transforms the architectural colors of the brownstone and the slate to the natural colors of the shining orange of the sun and the dark blue of the sky:

It is true:
in the light colors
of morning

brown-stone and slate
shine orange and dark blue.

As we have seen, the central metaphor of the poem concerns force: the steepletop ornament trying to hold back the lines of the steeple and the lines escaping. At this point, that central metaphor is picked up again:

But observe
the oppressive weight
of the squat edifice!
Observe
the jasmine lightness
of the moon.

Weight is a downward force; something heavy presses down on whatever is under it. The church is "squat." The choice of the word reflects its sound-symbolic value. "Squ-"

is an onset cluster that occurs in such words as "squeeze," "squish," "squash," and "squint," where it has the semantic value of "compression." The compression image evoked by "squat" reinforces the image of the church in the passage, which is one of oppressive weight. The downward force of the church is contrasted with "the jasmine lightness / of the moon." The moon floats above. The smell of jasmine blossoms near the ground floats upward to us. And the moon, as before, is the flower, here the jasmine flower.

A GLOBAL METAPHORICAL READING

So far, we have seen a variety of metaphors: conceptual mappings (e.g., seeing as touching, form as motion, events as actions) and image-mappings (e.g., the eaten moon, color mappings). Taken one by one, each of these is interesting and compelling in itself, but together they function in the service of a larger purpose. The poem, after all, is more than just instructions for looking at a church in early morning. The poem as a whole can be read as giving larger and more general instructions. Those who read the poem in this way may, of course, differ on just what larger and more general instructions the poem is suggesting. But they are all attributing to the poem a global metaphorical structure, that is, they are assuming that the poem presents a source domain which we are to map onto some target domain of larger concerns.

Global metaphorical readings are open in certain ways and constrained in others. Take the choice of target domain. The text or the title of the poem may indicate it overtly or may hint at it, but typically the reader has wide latitude in choosing a target domain. The main constraints are that the choice must "make sense" and the reading must be "justified." Not just any target domain and any reading will do. One constraint is that the mapping make use of conventional conceptual metaphors, that is, metaphors that exist in our conceptual system independent of any particular reading of a particular poem. Another constraint is the use of commonplace knowledge in conjunction with conventional metaphors. An additional constraint is iconicity—correspondences between form and meaning. If there is an iconic structure of the poem, it must cohere with the overall reading. The use of such constraints is part of what justifies an overall reading.

Not surprisingly, the poem lends itself to more than one such global metaphorical reading. For example, there is a possible reading of this poem in which the title, "To a Solitary Disciple," is taken as suggesting that the poet is addressing one of his own disciples, namely, an apprentice poet. Under that reading, the instructions in the poem are to be understood metaphorically as instructions concerning how a poet should go about looking at the world which is the subject of his poetry. We will not pursue this particular reading here.

The reading we will present is one in which the source domain is the primary reading we have given: an image of a church in the early morning and instructions on how to see and understand that image; the target domain is taken to be religion and instructions about the nature of religious belief and practice. Even with this restriction to a target domain, more than one justifiable reading may be possible. We will spend the rest of this chapter providing just one such reading.

The poem is titled "To a Solitary Disciple." A disciple, within a religious context, is commonly someone who is seeking the truths religion has to offer within the framework of a religious institution. Accordingly, the poem can be interpreted as addressing a disciple's principal concern— the search for religious truth. To do that, the poem as a whole would have to be interpreted metaphorically as a way to understand the nature of religious belief and practice (the target domain) in terms of a way of looking at a particular church in a particular natural setting (the source domain).

If we follow this reading of the title, we can see the poem as a set of instructions for the disciple, telling him how to look at the church metaphorically by looking at it physically. And it does so without ever saying anything overt about religion. How is this possible? The disciple is given instructions about what to see. How can such instructions be metaphorical? And how can they make sense as being about religion?

For the poem as a whole to be metaphorical, it must have a source and a target domain. The source domain concerns the *appearance* of a particular church. We propose that target domain concerns the *essence* of religion. For there to be such an interpretation, there must be a metaphorical link between appearances and essences.

The link arises in a way that is so natural that the only difficulty is in picking apart the details. An essence is that which makes something what it is; it is what cannot change without a loss of identity. It is therefore the most important thing about the nature of something. It is at this point that metaphor enters. Importance is understood metaphorically in the following way: IMPORTANT IS CENTRAL; LESS IMPORTANT IS PERIPHERAL, as in expressions like "Let's get to the heart of the matter," "What are the central points?," "We haven't yet delved deeply into the matter," "We uncovered an important truth," and so on. The immediate metaphorical inference is that ESSENCE IS CENTRAL. Both the essence and appearance are inalienable to the object, but the essence is more important. Add to that the commonplace knowledge that, typically, only the outsides of things are directly accessible to perception, and it follows that essences are not directly accessible to perception, while appearances, of course, are.

Since we can perceive the appearance but not the essence, the question arises, can we determine the essence of something from its appearance? There are two common and opposed answers among our cultural models. First, the appearance obscures the essence. Hence, we have phrases like "appearances are deceiving" and "you can't tell a book by its cover." Second, there is the contrary view that the appearance manifests the essence, so that close and accurate scrutiny of the appearance lets us come to know the nature of the essence. Hence, adages like "he's got an honest face" and "I don't like the look of him." There is, in addition, a third cultural model that resolves the apparent contradiction: only if one knows how to observe correctly will one determine the essence by looking at the appearance. As Blake writes, "A fool sees not the same tree that a wise man sees."

It is this third cultural model about the relation of appearance to essence that the metaphorical interpretation of the poem as a whole is based on.

In this poem, religious truth is the essence that the physical church houses. So if the disciple correctly observes the appearance of the church building, he will understand the essence of religious truth. Thus each passage is an instruction to observe. The entire poem is a tutorial in how to look at the appearance of the church in order to arrive at the proper understanding of the essence of religion. Recall the last stanza:

> But observe
> the oppressive weight
> of the squat edifice!
> Observe
> the jasmine lightness
> of the moon.

The "squat edifice" is the church building. Here there is a metonymy at work: THE BUILDING STANDS FOR THE IN-STITUTION, which we see in expressions such as "The White House is responsible for that policy," where the institution is the executive branch of government. By this metonymy, the church building stands for institutionalized Christianity. The "oppressive weight" can then be understood via the metaphor DIFFICULTIES ARE BURDENS, which is linked to other common metaphors, such as PURPOSES ARE DESTINATIONS and CONTROL IS UP and BEING CONTROLLED IS BEING KEPT DOWN. If you are trying to get somewhere, then carrying a heavy weight will make it harder to do so. Thus we have many common expressions which view difficulties in terms of weights: "My job is weighing me down," "Don't burden me with your problems," "Get off my back," and so on. Just as physical burdens keep one down physically, so metaphorical burdens are seen as constraints on freedom, which is metaphorically up, as in phrases like "Rise up and cast off your chains," "Slavery kept the blacks down," "Under the yoke of that oppressive regime, citizens had almost no liberties," and so on. Thus, the "oppressive weight / of the squat edifice" refers via metaphor and metonymy to the constraints imposed by institutionalized Christianity.

The last stanza contrasts oppressive institutional constraints with the "jasmine lightness of the moon." The smell of jasmine comes from something living, a fragile flower, as opposed to something abstract and institutionalized, like religious dogma. The smell of jasmine is light, rising upward from the ground, not heavy and earthbound. Metaphorically, it represents freedom; there is nothing holding it down, just as there is nothing holding down the moon.

The poem indeed begins by pointing out that the moon is above the church. "Rather notice, mon cher, / that the moon is / tilted above / the point of the steeple." Why does a church have a steeple? While the church is earthbound, the steeple rises up and points toward the divine, that is, to what the church exists to serve. A steeple is thus a physical embodiment of a religious metaphor, namely DIVINE IS UP; MORTAL IS DOWN. Thus, the soul ascends to heaven while the body goes down into the grave. In the source domain, the moon is physically above the point of the steeple; metaphorically, in the target domain, the divine is more important than the institution of the church. An instruction to the disciple to notice that the moon lies above the steeple point is thus metaphorically an instruction to understand that the institution of the church is less important than the divine. Looking just at the church, without noticing its relation to the moon, would be a mistake; and focusing on the institution of the church, without concentrating on its relation to the divine, would be the wrong way to understand religious truth.

But there is more to the relationship between the moon and the church than that the moon is above the church: the steeple additionally *points toward* the moon. We can understand the relationship *points toward* metaphorically by bringing to bear a further basic metaphor that reinforces the DIVINE IS UP metaphor evoked by the up-down relationship, as follows: in the visual field, we actually point toward what deserves attention. We understand that the eye can focus on just one area, and that when something else deserves attention, we must redirect the gaze of the viewer from wherever he is looking to that which deserves attention. We do this by pointing. There is a metaphoric understanding of mental attention, called THE MIND'S EYE METAPHOR, through which we understand the attention of the mind to some topic in terms of the direction of the visual gaze at some locus. Thus we say, "We need to shift perspective," "His insight into this problem is blocked by his own big ego," "He was looking in the wrong place for a solution," and so on. Via this metaphor, redirecting the mind from one topic to a more important one is understood in terms of pointing from the current locus of visual attention to another, more important visual locus. This allows us to understand the relationship *points toward* in the following way: if the physical church is metonymic for institutionalized religion, then seeing the steeple of the church pointing at the moon above it can be, metaphorically, seeing institutionalized religion as "pointing toward" something more important above it, namely the moon, which we can understand as the divine through DIVINE IS UP.

In the description of what the disciple is to see, we find that he is instructed to avoid seeing the lines of the church building as being contained by the edifice. On the contrary, he must see these lines as rising above that edifice. He is to see that the most important aspect of these lines is not that they configure the church building but rather that they rise above it to flank and contain the moon. This set of instructions concerns the source domain, the image of the church building. Metaphorically, they concern the target domain, the nature of religious truth and value: the institution of the church exists to protect and guard the divine, to be the custodian of what is most valuable. The lines of church dogma and practice are thus not important in themselves. Their ultimate purpose is not to provide a structure for the institution. On the contrary, their ultimate purpose is to protect and guard and serve the divine. To see the relation between the lines of the church steeple and the moon is to understand metaphorically the proper relation between institutional structure and religious value.

The disciple is further to observe not just that the lines of the steeple rise up to flank the moon but that these lines are the sepals of a flower, and the moon is the bloom. Again, this is an instruction about the source domain, about what the disciple is to observe about the visual scene. How do we understand this instruction as referring metaphorically to the target domain of religious value? If the lines of the steeple are seen merely as geometric lines, then they are inanimate, unchanging, abstract, hard, insensate, impersonal, and lacking in higher purpose. But if they form part of a flower, protecting the center of the flower, then they are animate, organic, sensitive, soft, particular, and have the higher purpose of protecting and guarding something fragile. Moreover, a building is constructed by man, but a flower is made by God. Similarly, if the moon is just a heavenly body in the sky, then it certainly needs no protection and is served by nothing. It is mere inorganic material, inanimate and insensitive. But if the moon is the center of the flower, then it is fragile, animate, and in need of protection. It is vital and can emit a beautiful, ethereal fragrance. To see the lines of the church as forming the protective sepal is therefore to see the higher purpose of the institution as serving the sensitive, fragile, precious, living, divine part of the individual. The higher purpose of the general institution is to guard and support particular souls in their relation to the divine.

We are now in a position to return to a very telling detail about the first description of the moon in this poem. The disciple is instructed to see not only that the moon is above the steeple but also that it is *tilted* above that steeple. What does this say about the target domain of the nature of religion and the divine? Notice that the lines of the steeple form a hexagon, that is, a regular, symmetrical, perfect, balanced, abstract shape. But the moon is tilted, tipped in one direction as opposed to another. It is thus asymmetrical. This sets up an opposition between the moon and the frozen lines of the steeple which is resolved only if the disciple sees the lines of the steeple as escaping the static, perfect hexagon and moving to embrace the asymmetry of the moon.

This opposition is understood in terms of a very basic metaphor, PERFECT IS REGULAR; IMPERFECT IS IRREGU-LAR. We say of something perfect that it is "without a blemish," which means that there is no irregular spot in it. We also say that it is "spotless" or "flawless" or "immaculate." We can say that behavior is less than perfect by calling it "highly irregular." We also have the commonplace knowledge that anything in the real world is at least slightly irregular. No line in the real world is absolutely straight, and all living things have bumps and spots and incongruities and asymmetries. When we combine the metaphor IMPER-FECT IS IRREGULAR with the knowledge that real things are irregular, this entails, metaphorically, that living things are inherently imperfect, while abstract, nonreal ideas can be perfect.

Thus, an instruction to see the moon as irregular, as asymmetrical, is an instruction to see, metaphorically, that the essence of the divine, which the church is to serve and protect, is not the abstract, perfect, lifeless doctrine of the institution, but rather real, imperfect, vital beings.

This same entailment that the real is imperfect helps us understand the second stanza:

> Rather observe
> that it is early morning
> than that the sky
> is smooth
> as a turquoise.

The disciple is instructed not to attend principally to the smoothness of the sky. Smoothness is tactile regularity, perfection. On the contrary, he is to attend principally to the fact that it is early morning, which is to say, to a particular time which is unlike the other times around it, and which is changeable, not eternal. This further explains why he is to see the lines of the church steeple as moving, dynamic, changing, and thus real and live. And it explains why the disciple is to see that the lines of the steeple change into a sepal—that the static, abstract geometric hexagon is to become a curved natural shape.

What the disciple is to notice principally are relationships between the church and the divine: he is to notice that the moon is *above* the steeple, and *tilted*; he is to notice that the lines of the steeple rise up and embrace the moon, that they flank it, contain it, and guard it; he is to notice that the moon lies in the protecting lines. He is to notice that while the weight of the edifice presses downward, the jasmine lightness of the moon remains above. All of this concerns relationships. He is to notice only to a lesser degree the colors of the scene: the shell-pink of the moon, the turquoise color of the sky, the way the brown-stone and slate become orange and dark blue. But the poet points out that, though less important, the colors are still there to be noticed: "It is true: / in the light colors / of morning / brownstone and slate / shine orange and dark blue." What sort of colors is the disciple to notice, if he is to notice them at all? He is to notice the pink of a shell, the blue of a turquoise, the orange of the sun, and the dark blue of the sky, that is, colors of things naturally occuring in the real, imperfect world. He is to notice that the colors of manufactured things—the cut brown-stone and slate building materials—are transformed in the scene into natural colors.

The last instruction to the disciple is, "Observe / the jasmine lightness / of the moon." This instruction embodies all the instructions. The word "observe" has two meanings: "to look at" and "to conform to," as in a ritual. It is at once an instruction for looking at the church, an instruction for understanding the true nature of religion, and, most important, an instruction for practicing that understanding. "Jasmine" and "moon" recall the image of the flower superimposed on the moon—metaphorically the essence of the divine which is above the institution of the church. A color mapping reinforces the superimposition of the flower on the moon: the "lightness" of the moon is the color of the jasmine flower. "Lightness" is also buoyancy; it suggests an upward motion like the scent of jasmine rising from the ground, in opposition to the oppressive weight of the institutional church. The lightness recalls the upward force of the lines escaping.

The ultimate instruction to the disciple is to transcend, to rise above, the institution. This is conveyed metaphorically in the central image of the poem in which the lines rise above the steeple that is ordinarily seen as "containing" them. Transcendence, motion beyond the ordinary limits, is also conveyed in the very structure of the sentence that describes the image of transcendence.

The instructions to the disciple are all given in a single form: they oppose what he should principally observe against what he should only secondarily observe. Each instruction also has a sentence structure mirroring that opposition: "Rather notice x than y," "Rather observe x than y," "It is true that y, but observe x and z." The instruction to see the lines as transcending the steeple begins with the same pattern: "Rather grasp. . . ." But just as the lines of the steeple escape the pattern of the steeple, so the words decribing the escape themselves escape the expected sentence structure. Just when we would expect the second half, the "than" half, we find that the first half overflows, so that there is no second half presenting an opposition.

> Rather grasp
> how the dark
> converging lines
> of the steeple
> meet at the pinnacle—
> perceive how
> its little ornament
> tries to stop them—
>
> See how it fails!
> See how the converging lines
> of the hexagonal spire
> escape upward—

We expect the "Rather grasp" to be followed by a "than" clause. But instead, the primary instruction continues on. "Perceive . . ." "See how it fails!" Thus the sentence in which the disciple is instructed to see how the lines extend beyond their conventional bounds itself extends beyond its conventional bounds.

The mapping between the structure of this sentence and the structure of the image of escape is an image-mapping based on the metaphor FORM IS MOTION. Sentences and clauses are forms. By FORM IS MOTION, these sentences and clauses are understood as moving, as when we say "This sentence runs on too long," "This paragraph flows nicely," "That paragraph stops abruptly," and so on. Through this metaphor, each clause has a motion which stops when the clause ends. The motion of the "rather" clause would normally be stopped by the beginning of the "than" clause, but it is not. It continues on. The meaning of the "than" clause would normally be opposed to the meaning of the "rather" clause. But here the opposition is overridden.

The image of the steeple also has a form, which is understood metaphorically as the same motion: the linear form is a linear motion which normally stops where the lines meet, but in this case it does not. The lines go on. Though the form of the sentence and the form of the steeple are two very different kinds of form, we can understand them metaphorically as motions having the same overall shape. The image-mapping between the sentence and the image that it conveys is as follows: the linear form of the "rather" clause maps onto the linear form of the steeple lines; the metaphorical linear motion of the clause maps onto the metaphorical linear motion of the steeple lines; the expected metaphorical stoppage of the "rather" clause at the "than" clause maps onto the expected metaphorical stoppage of the steeple lines at the ornament where they meet; the metaphorical opposing force of the meaning of the "than" clause maps onto the metaphorical opposing force of the ornament; and the continued motion of the "rather" clause past its expected stopping point maps onto the continued motion of the steeple lines past their expected stopping point.

What we have here is an image-mapping based on structure—in this case, structure that is in part metaphorically imposed. When such a mapping exists between the structure of a sentence and the structure of the meaning or the image that the sentence conveys, the mapping is called "iconic." This is, in general, what iconicity in language is: a metaphorical image-mapping in which the structure of the meaning is understood in terms of the structure of the form of the language presenting that meaning. Such mappings are possible because of the existence of image-schemas, such as schemas characterizing bounded spaces (with interiors and exteriors), paths, motions along those paths, forces, parts and wholes, centers and peripheries, and so on. When we speak of the "form of language," we are understanding that form in terms of such image-schemas. Thus, for example, one aspect of sentence structure is given in terms of parts and wholes, that is, the parts of speech and the higher-level constituents containing them. Other aspects of a sentence's structure are given in terms of balance, proximity, subordination, sequence, and so on. The schematic images that allow us to understand such syntactic notions are also used in conceptual structure. It is for this reason that image-schematic correspondences between form and meaning are possible. The mechanism that relates them is the same mapping mechanism used in metaphor.

An iconic mapping of the same kind also relates the form of the poem as a whole to the meaning of the poem as a whole. Recall the principle image of the poem, in which the lines of the steeple escape past the ornament. The ornament, the point at which the lines meet and continue on, lies at the center of the visual image. The sentence in which that is described, "See how it fails," occurs in the center of the poem as a whole. And the spiritual transcendence that is conveyed metaphorically in terms of this image is the most important, and therefore metaphorically central, instruction of the poem about religious values.

Iconicity provides an extra layer of metaphorical structure to the poem. As we have seen, the religious meaning of the poem is understood metaphorically in terms of the images. The iconic layer is the mapping from the structure of the language to the structure of the image presented and to the overall meaning of the poem. Our intuition about the degree of organic unity of a poem is based on our unconscious recognition of just such coherences between the formal and conceptual aspects of the poem.

In fact, we can see yet one more layer of coherent metaphorical interpretation at the center of the poem. The center of the poem—where the ornament fails to stop the lines—is the point at which the disciple is instructed to let his imagination "break free" to see things that one could not in conventional fashion see in the visual field. The movement of the lines and their stoppage can be seen conventionally through FORM IS MOTION, but to see the lines break past the conventional boundary is to let imagination take over from conventional perception. There is a metaphoric understanding of the workings of imagination that is based on motion, via the metaphor that THE MIND IS A BODY MOVING IN SPACE, and the related metaphor that KNOWING IS SEEING. In the first metaphor, the mind is following a mental path to its goal, as when we say, "Follow the path of the argument," "The logic leads in this direction," and so on. Mental progress stops when the mind is blocked on its path, and a new mental path is needed. Imagination is the formation of an image, something that the mind can "see," and which therefore provides a form of knowledge. Imagination can be understood via this metaphor as the power to arrive at knowledge by constructing an image, say, an image that allows one to overcome blockage by reperceiving the situation unconventionally. We say, for example, "Use your imagination to find some way around this impasse." Thus, the linear form of the "rather" clause running past its conventional stopping point can additionally be iconic of the movement of the imagination past the conventional limits of perception.

We began this book by referring to the commonplace notion that poetic language is beyond ordinary language, something possessing special instruments of its own. We have been arguing that, on the contrary, poetic language uses the same conceptual and linguistic apparatus as ordinary language. In this poem we have seen the use of extremely common conventional metaphors like FORM IS MOTION, EVENTS ARE ACTIONS and IMPORTANT IS CENTRAL. It is in part because these metaphors are part of our ordinary mode of thought that the poem can have the power that it does.

In chapter two we separated out various ways in which poetry can use our common metaphoric conceptualizations powerfully. First, these conceptualizations are powerful because they are automatic, unconscious, and hence effortless. We see the poet here using this sort of power when he describes the sky as "smooth" and the lines as "converging" and "meeting." Our automatic use of SEEING IS TOUCHING and FORM IS MOTION make these expressions so natural that we do not even notice their metaphoric nature.

Another dimension of poetic power is the power to compose basic metaphors. We see the poet use this power when he characterizes the lines as "escaping": this composes FORM IS MOTION and EVENTS ARE ACTIONS with the knowledge that moving things have force. Perhaps the most salient of the dimensions of poetic power used in this poem is the power to extend basic metaphors. The lines cannot escape unless they are already in motion, converging and meeting. Unless "converging" and "meeting" are understood metaphorically in terms of FORM IS MOTION, there can be no metaphoric extension of the motion.

Such uses of metaphor are local. But the major effect of metaphor in this poem is global—the interpretation of the entire description of the scene as a statement about the nature of religion. Here we find a power of metaphor that we have not previously discussed, *the power of revelation*. This is the power that metaphor has to reveal comprehensive hidden meanings to us, to allow us to find meanings beyond the surface, to interpret texts as wholes, and to make sense of patterns of events.

It is important to see, however, that all the detailed analysis we have given does not constitute a literary-critical treatment of the poem. Various literary critics concern themselves with reading a poem by bringing to bear a host of issues: the poem's historical context, the biography, dialect, politics, or profession of the author, the tradition the poem comes from, the way it is influenced by previous poems in that tradition, the genre of the poem, the connotations of particular words like "edifice" as opposed to "moon," the ways and reasons poets get published or ignored, the issue of reputation and canonization of the author and his tradition, issues of gender, and so on. What we are concerned to provide throughout this book is instead a prerequisite to any such discussion, namely, a linguistic and rhetorical analysis of the role of metaphor in the way we understand a poem.

FOUR

The Great Chain of Being

Proverbs as Poems

Poetry has the power to instruct us in what to notice, how to understand, and how to conduct our lives. Proverbs are often viewed as the simplest form of such poetry.

In this chapter, we will investigate basic mechanisms of poetry which appear in high relief in proverbs but which suffuse all our poetry. Let us consider, for a moment, as an introduction to these mechanisms, three lines that Yeats, in his poem "Under Ben Bulben," suggests as the epitaph for his tombstone:

> Cast a cold eye
> On life, on death.
> Horseman, pass by!

Certain features of these lines will surface repeatedly as we look at proverbs. They evoke a vivid image of a source domain—a horseman who is to ride past the tombstone he encounters on his way. And yet we understand intuitively and automatically that more than a particular horseman or tombstone is being commented upon. Somehow, from the line "On life, on death" we know to take this directive to the horseman as telling us something about how to conduct our lives. What it tells us and how we know this are our subjects here.

Questions such as these—what are we being told? and how do we know that?—arise with least distraction in proverbs. Let us look at some translations of proverbs by W. S. Merwin in *Asian Figures*:

Charcoal
writes everybody's name
black

Blind
blames the ditch

Big thunder
little rain

Jelly
in a vise

Not big
but a pepper

Cows run with the wind
horses against it

Cow
parched by the sun
pants at the moon

Burned lips on broth
now blows on cold water

Frog
forgets he had a tail

Cow in the stream
eating from both banks

Knife can't whittle
its own handle

Any weather
chicken's
pants are rolled up

The rats decide
the cat ought to be belled

Ants on a millstone
whichever way they walk
they go around with it

These poems are instructions for understanding the nature
of our being, the nature of people and situations we encounter, and our role in the universe. In each case, the instructions are addressed metaphorically. The presumption
is that higher-order questions are answered in terms of
lower-order descriptions: the human place in the universe

in terms of ants on a millstone, human slander in terms of the properties of charcoal, human character in terms of the behavior of cows and horses, the general response to one's inadequacies in terms of the particular response of a blind man in a ditch.

Moreover, these poems give very general instructions that can apply to a wide range of situations, but not just any situation. How do we understand these poems as making these comments about people? How do we understand these poems as having general meanings?

The Generic Is Specific Metaphor

Proverbs evoke schemas rich in images and information: they evoke knowledge of common animals, objects, and situations. These schemas, which we referred to in chapter two as "specific-level schemas," include not only generic-level information such as causal relations and shapes of events but also specific details and concrete images. In understanding a proverb like

> Blind
> blames the ditch

we use such specific-level schemas.

This proverb is understood as being not just about blind people but about a broader class of people, people who have some incapacity. How is this possible? How can a statement about a particular situation convey a general understanding? And how do we know what general understanding it conveys?

There is a general answer to these questions for all poetry with the characteristics of this proverb. There exists a single generic-level metaphor, GENERIC IS SPECIFIC, which maps a single specific-level schema onto an indefinitely large number of parallel specific-level schemas that all have the same generic-level structure as the source-domain schema.

This metaphor, like other generic-level metaphors, has variable source and target domains. It restricts source and target domains only by requiring that the source be a specific-level schema and the target be a generic-level schema. The mapping of GENERIC IS SPECIFIC, rather than being defined by a fixed list of elements, is defined by the constraint that governs all generic-level metaphors, namely, that it preserve the generic-level structure of the target domain, except for what the metaphor exists explicitly to change, and import as much generic-level structure of the source domain as is consistent with that first constraint. But in the case of GENERIC IS SPECIFIC, the metaphor exists to change none of the generic-level structure of the target domain. Consequently, the constraint on generic-level metaphors becomes, in the case of GENERIC IS SPECIFIC, equivalent to requiring that the source and target have the same generic-level structure. In other words, GENERIC IS SPECIFIC maps specific-level schemas onto the generic-level schemas they contain. These are the fewest restrictions possible for a metaphorical mapping, resulting in a metaphorical mapping of extreme generality.

Consider an example of how GENERIC IS SPECIFIC allows us to understand a proverb as used in a particular situation. Suppose a presidential candidate knowingly commits some personal impropriety (though not illegal and not related to political issues), and his candidacy is destroyed by the press's reporting of the impropriety. He blames the press for reporting it rather than himself for committing it. Suppose we think he should have recognized the realities of political press coverage when he chose to commit the impropriety. We express our judgment by saying, "Blind / blames the ditch."

From the schema associated with "Blind / blames the ditch," we pick out just the generic-level information, which is as follows:

— There is a person with an incapacity.
— He encounters a situation in which his incapacity in that situation results in a negative consequence.
— He blames the situation rather than his own incapacity.
— He should have held himself responsible, not the situation.

This extracted generic-level information constitutes a generic-level schema, which can be instantiated by many other

specific-level schemas. Thus we can think of it as a variable template that can be filled in in many ways. Here is one way:
— The person is the presidential candidate.
— His incapacity is his inability to understand the consequences of his own improper actions.
— The context he encounters is his knowingly committing an impropriety and the press's reporting it.
— The consequence is having his candidacy dashed.
— He blames the press.
— We judge him as being foolish for blaming the press instead of himself.

This leads us to the following specific-level metaphoric understanding of the given situation:
— The blind person corresponds to the presidential candidate.
— His blindness corresponds to his inability to understand the consequences of his own actions.
— Falling into the ditch corresponds to his committing the impropriety and having it reported.
— Being in the ditch corresponds to being out of the running as a candidate.
— Blaming the ditch corresponds to blaming the press coverage.
— Judging the blind man as foolish for blaming the ditch corresponds to judging the candidate as foolish for blaming the press coverage.

Thus, applying the generic-level metaphor GENERIC IS SPECIFIC to the first specific-level schema (the one evoked by the proverb) lets us extract a generic-level schema that can be instantiated by some second specific-level schema, thereby creating a species-level metaphor connecting the first and second species-level schemas.

GENERIC IS SPECIFIC is a generic-level metaphor of the sort we discussed in chapter two. As such, it preserves the generic-level structure of the target domain, except for what the metaphor exists explicitly to change—in this case nothing—and imports as much as possible of the generic-level structure of the source domain—in this case everything. As a generic-level metaphor, it is a variable metaphor in the sense that it guides and constrains the imaginative construction of a range of specific-level metaphorical mappings.

The GENERIC IS SPECIFIC metaphor thus allows us to understand a whole category of situations in terms of one particular situation. Given a particular situation (say, the presidential candidate) and a particular proverb (say, "Blind / blames the ditch"), GENERIC IS SPECIFIC provides a way of understanding that situation metaphorically in terms of the schema evoked by the proverb.

Additionally, in the absence of any particular situation (say, when we are reading a list of proverbs like the one above), we can nonetheless understand the proverb metaphorically via the GENERIC IS SPECIFIC metaphor. The reason is that, in the absence of any particular specific-level target schema, the generic-level schema of the source domain counts as an acceptable target. That generic-level schema can fit a range of possible specific-level target schemas, and so, when we read a proverb in isolation, we can muse over a range of particular situations to which it applies.

Generic-level schemas have the power of generality, that is, the power to make sense of a wide range of cases. But they lack the power of specificity. Specific-level schemas are both concrete and information-rich: they have rich imagery associated with them, they are memorable, they are connected to our everyday experiences, and they contain a relatively large amount of information about those concrete everyday experiences. Proverbs use both kinds of power: they lead us to general characterizations, which nevertheless are grounded in the richness of the special case.

Such specific-level schemas tend to be evoked by short, common words, like "blind," "blame," and "ditch." As a result, short proverbs tend to be packed with information and imagery. Consequently, the knowledge they call up includes a great deal of generic-level information as well as specific-level information. For this reason, the GENERIC IS SPECIFIC metaphor, applied to a short proverb, picks out a lot of generic-level information—information that could not be expressed at all concisely using abstract generic-level language.

For example, take the proverb

> Burned lips on broth
> now blows on cold water.

We understand this by isolating the generic-level schema contained in the specific-level schema evoked:

> A traumatic experience can lead to an automatic response to all situations even remotely similar, even when the response is completely inappropriate.

Compared to the proverb, this is lengthy and dull. It lacks the powerful images and rich knowledge of burned lips, broth, blowing, and cold water.

Of course, GENERIC IS SPECIFIC applies to proverbs worldwide, not just to Asian figures. We might have discussed "The girl who can't dance says the band can't play" instead of "Blind / blames the ditch," or "Once bitten, twice shy" instead of "Burned lips on broth / now blows on cold water." We surmise that the distinction between generic-level information and specific-level information is common in conceptual systems throughout the world and that proverbs are common in the world's cultures because of this distinction.

The Great Chain

What is taken for granted in proverbs is that we have a certain sense of the order of things, that we know a great deal about man's place in the universe. Proverbs concern people, though they often look superficially as if they concern other things—cows, frogs, peppers, knives, charcoal. We understand proverbs as offering us ways of comprehending the complex faculties of human beings in terms of these other things. To do this, we use the Great Chain of Being.

The Great Chain of Being is a cultural model that concerns kinds of beings and their properties and places them on a vertical scale with "higher" beings and properties above "lower" beings and properties. When we talk about man's "higher" faculties, we mean his aesthetic and moral sense and rational capacity, not his physical characteristics, his animal desires, or his raw emotions. We speak of higher and lower forms of life. The Great Chain is a scale of forms of being—human, animal, plant, inanimate object—and consequently a scale of the properties that characterize forms of being—reason, instinctual behavior, biological function, physical attributes, and so on.

Commonly, the Great Chain of Being is taught as background to literature and the history of ideas, as essential to an understanding of the worldviews of classical authors like Plato and Aristotle, medieval authors like Dante and Chaucer, Renaissance authors like Shakespeare, and even Augustan authors like Pope. But it is taught as if it somehow died out in the industrial age. On the contrary, a highly articulated version of it still exists as a contemporary unconscious cultural model indispensable to our understanding of ourselves, our world, and our language.

We will distinguish between two versions of the Great Chain, one basic and one extended. The basic Great Chain concerns the relation of human beings to "lower" forms of existence. It is extremely widespread and occurs not only in Western culture but throughout a wide range of the world's cultures. It is largely unconscious and so fundamental to our thinking that we barely notice it. The extended Great Chain concerns the relation of human beings to society, God, and the universe. The extended Great Chain is central to the Western tradition, and it is the main concern of traditional discussions of the Great Chain. We will consider the extended Great Chain later and concentrate for the moment on the basic Great Chain.

We think of humans as higher-order beings than animals, animals as higher than plants, and plants as higher than inanimate substances. Within each of these levels, there are higher and lower sublevels, so that dogs are higher-order beings than insects, and trees higher than algae. This scale of beings embodies a scale of properties. While a rock is mere substance, a chair additionally has a part-whole functional structure, that is, it has a seat, a back, and legs, each of which serves some function. A tree has both substance and part-whole functional structure, and in addition it has life. An insect has all of these properties—substance, a complex functional structure, life—and in addition animal behavior such as self-propulsion. According to our common-place knowledge, higher animals like dogs have all of these properties plus interior states such as desires (like wanting to play), emotions (like fear), limited cognitive abilities (like memory), and so on. Humans have all these properties plus capacities for abstract reasoning, aesthetics, morality, com-munication, highly developed consciousness, and so on. Thus, where a being falls in the scale of beings depends strictly on its highest property.

In the cultural model comprising the basic Great Chain, part of any being's nature is shared with lower beings. For example, it is not our instincts that separate us from beasts, because beasts also have instincts. It is the basic Great Chain that makes it sensible for us to speak of *our* "bestial in-stincts" and *our* "animal drives." Though we are not beasts, we share these properties with beasts and not with trees or algae. They are called "bestial instincts" because such in-stincts are a property that beasts and beings above them have while lower-order beings don't.

At any level in the basic Great Chain, the highest prop-erties of beings at that level characterize those beings. For example, the highest level properties of animals are their instincts. Forms of being at lower levels (e.g., amoebas, trees, chairs, rocks) do not have instincts. Although dif-ferent animals have different instinctive attributes and be-havior, nonetheless they all have some particular instincts. Therefore, instinct is a generic-level parameter of animals. Similarly, the mental, the moral, and the aesthetic are generic-level parameters of human beings; though different people have different mental capacities and different moral and aesthetic sensibilities, all human beings nonetheless have some of these or other. Thus, there is a generic-level characterization of our implicit unconscious cultural model of the basic Great Chain, a characterization that does not distinguish among kinds of humans, among kinds of higher animals, among kinds of lower animals, among kinds of plants, and so on. What defines a level are the attributes and behaviors distinguishing it from the next level below.

In the cultural model of the basic Great Chain, the attributes and behavior that define a given level are beyond those possessed by forms of being at lower levels. They are "beyond" in several senses. They are additional, that is, simply something *more* that lower forms do not have. They are more complex. They are more powerful, in the sense that they enable forms of being at that level to dominate forms of being at lower levels. Finally, the higher a distinguishing attribute is on the basic Great Chain, the less generally accessible it is to our perception and our understanding. For example, it is in general harder to determine a person's moral sense than an animal's predatory instincts because the human being can disguise that sense and because we cannot reliably infer that sense purely from the person's behavior. Animals do not hide their instinctive nature, and we can reliably determine that nature by observing their behavior. Similarly, it is harder to determine an animal's instinctive nature than it is to determine the physical attibutes of a rock, because determining instinctive nature requires that we deduce rationally that nature from our observations over time, while the physical attributes of rocks are directly accessible to our sensory perception.

THE NATURE OF THINGS

We have a commonplace theory of forms of being—that they have essences and that these essences lead to the way they behave or function. For example, we understand substances as having essential attributes such as *hard, soft, brittle,* and so on. We understand further that these essential physical attributes result in essential physical behavior; for example, heavy things resist movement and brittle things shatter. Some physical objects also have structural attributes. For example, barbed wire, which is metallic and therefore hard, also has a part-whole structure consisting of the wire and the barbs. Such an essential structural attribute determines how the barbed wire will function; for example, it can stretch across the range and prick animals that encounter it, or it can stretch across the top of a wall and prick those who try to climb over the wall.

Plants additionally have essential biological natures which

lead to essential biological behavior, as when a deciduous tree drops its leaves or a flower phototropically follows the sun. Higher animals additionally have essential instinctive natures which lead to essential instinctive behavior, as when a natural predator like an eagle hunts. Human beings have essential character attributes that determine characteristic behavior, as when a dishonest person characteristically lies.

Not all attributes are understood as being immutable and essential. They may be temporary or accidental. An animal may be at various moments hungry, fierce, sleepy, calm, and so on. A physical object may be at various times hot or cold, clean or dirty, new or old. And a human being may be at various moments gentle, angry, or phlegmatic. Just as essential attributes lead to essential behavior, so temporary attributes lead to temporary behavior. A human being temporarily angry, a dog temporarily provoked, and a kettle of water temporarily heated all behave in predictable ways.

In summary, we have a largely unconscious, automatic, commonplace theory about the nature of things, that is, the relationship between what things are like and how they behave:
— The attributes that a form of being has lead to the way that form of being behaves.
— Essential attributes lead to essential behavior.
— Contingent attributes lead to contingent behavior.
We will refer to this commonplace theory of the relationship between attributes and behavior as the Nature of Things.

The Great Chain Metaphor

The basic Great Chain is defined by attributes and behavior, arranged in a hierarchy:

The Basic Great Chain

— HUMANS: Higher-order attributes and behavior (e.g. thought, character)
— ANIMALS: Instinctual attributes and behavior
— PLANTS: Biological attributes and behavior

— COMPLEX OBJECTS: Structural attributes and functional behavior
— NATURAL PHYSICAL THINGS: Natural physical attributes and natural physical behavior

Each form of being has all of the attribute types lower on the hierarchy. For example, animals do not have mental and character attributes, but in addition to instinctual attributes they have biological, structural, and natural physical attributes.

The commonsense theory of the Nature of Things is a causal theory that links attributes to behavior: the characteristic behavior of a form of being is a consequence of its characteristic attributes. When the hierarchy of the basic Great Chain is combined with the commonplace knowledge about the Nature of Things, we get a more elaborated, hierarchical folk theory of forms of being and how they behave. From here on, until we begin our discussion of the extended Great Chain, we will refer to the basic Great Chain as simply the "Great Chain."

The Nature Of Things Plus The Great Chain

— HUMANS: Higher-order attributes lead to higher-order behavior.
— ANIMALS: Instinctual attributes lead to instinctual behavior.
— PLANTS: Biological attributes lead to biological behavior.
— COMPLEX OBJECTS: Structural attributes lead to functional behavior.
— NATURAL PHYSICAL THINGS: Natural physical attributes lead to natural physical behavior.

The commonsense theory of the Nature of Things combines with the Great Chain to form a complex commonsense theory of how things work in the world. This theory, as we will see, is an essential ingredient in the understanding of proverbs. There are two other essential ingredients:
— The GENERIC IS SPECIFIC metaphor.
— The communicative Maxim of Quantity: Be as informative as is required and not more so.

Though each of these four ingredients exists independently of the others, they are employed in concert to provide interpretations of proverbs. We will refer to the four, taken together, as the GREAT CHAIN METAPHOR. The GREAT CHAIN METAPHOR is thus an ensemble, something like a string quartet, in which there are four members with separate identities, but who so often play together that their identity as a group is more prominent than their identities as individuals. Still it is important to bear in mind that the GREAT CHAIN METAPHOR is not, strictly speaking, a metaphor alone. It is an ensemble consisting of the commonsense theory of the Nature of Things + the Great Chain + the GENERIC IS SPECIFIC metaphor + the Maxim of Quantity. What makes it metaphoric in character is the GENERIC IS SPECIFIC metaphor. The Nature of Things + the Great Chain give it the character of a commonsense theory. And the Maxim of Quantity builds into it a pragmatic principle of communication. In this sense, the GREAT CHAIN METAPHOR is more than just a metaphor: it is a recurring conceptual complex made up of a metaphor, a commonsense theory, and a communicative principle.

Because it is a conceptual complex of this kind, the GREAT CHAIN METAPHOR is a tool of great power and scope. By linking the Great Chain with the GENERIC IS SPECIFIC metaphor, it allows us to comprehend general human character traits in terms of well-understood nonhuman attributes; and, conversely, it allows us to comprehend less well-understood aspects of the nature of animals and objects in terms of better-understood human characteristics.

The reason that the GREAT CHAIN METAPHOR is so powerful in scope is that it applies to our overall knowledge of everything in the Great Chain, from human beings down to inanimate physical objects. The schemas that characterize our knowledge about people are separate from our schemas that characterize our knowledge of the physical world. The Great Chain allows us to link such disparate schemas, and the GENERIC IS SPECIFIC metaphor picks out from such specific schemas common generic-level structure. Such common structure defines new conceptual categories in which the human and the nonhuman are seen as instances of the same thing.

Because we have so much knowledge, this process would go haywire were it not for the Maxim of Quantity. Its role is to limit severely what can be understood in terms of what. Because the Great Chain is an implicational hierarchy, where "higher" forms of being have all the kinds of properties that "lower" forms of being have, we apply the Maxim of Quantity on this linear hierarchy so as to pick out the highest-ranking properties available in each situation. This happens as follows: when a speaker refers to something at one level of the Great Chain, we assume that it is the properties that define that level that are of interest; for if only lower properties were of interest, then the speaker would, in referring to this higher-level being, have given us a great deal of superfluous information to sort through, namely, all the higher properties defining that higher level. This means that the speaker would have violated the Maxim of Quantity—he or she would have given us too much information. Since we assume that the speaker is not violating the Maxim of Quantity, we must assume that it is the highest ranking properties that are of interest. For example, if the speaker wishes us to pay attention to functional part-whole structure only, then he or she can refer to something having functional part-whole structure as its highest level of property, such as a pair of pliers, or a vise. If the speaker were to refer instead to an animal, without telling us explicitly to look at the functional part-whole structure of the animal, then he or she would have given us a wealth of superfluous information, namely all the higher properties that distinguish animals from complex objects. The speaker would have violated the Maxim of Quantity by giving us too much information. We assume that the speaker is not violating the Maxim of Quantity; and so we must assume that the properties of interest are the highest ranking properties characterizing the level of the animal. The Maxim of Quantity thus places extremely strong constraints on the application of the Great Chain + GENERIC IS SPECIFIC. The result is that the conceptual complex we are calling the

GREAT CHAIN METAPHOR, though powerful, is limited. The best way to appreciate both its power and its limitations is to look carefully at examples.

Consider the proverb

> Big thunder
> little rain

This statement concerns a particular natural event with two sub-events, thundering and raining. Like all the proverbs we discuss, it captures a vivid, memorable, concrete image of a source domain, but it does not explicitly mention the target domain. Nothing in the words "Big thunder / little rain" mentions people, or human events.

It is thus unlike most of the poetic metaphors we have so far discussed. For example, consider Dickinson's poetic lines, based on the metaphor DEATH IS DEPARTURE:

> Because I could not stop for Death—
> He kindly stopped for me—
> The Carriage held but just Ourselves—
> And Immortality

These lines use words referring both to the source domain of departure ("stopped for me," "Carriage") and to the target domain of death ("Death," "Immortality"). By contrast, the proverb "Big thunder / little rain" uses words referring to the source domain (the natural event of storms), but no words referring to the target domain (human events).

How do we know that such a proverb refers to the human sphere, so that we can apply the GREAT CHAIN METAPHOR? First, notice that it is not absolutely necessary to interpret this proverb as referring to the domain of things human. It *could*, in the right context, be simply a description of an individual storm. But in that case, we would somehow know that it is not functioning as a proverb. Second, notice that we might know it is about human things from the context of the discourse in which it occurs. If we are asked by a friend to say what a new acquaintance is like, and we respond "Big thunder / little rain," then the friend already knows that our answer is almost certainly a remark about the acquaintance. In that case, the discourse situation indicates the target domain and that we are to understand the utterance as a proverbial remark about a person.

But suppose we encounter the proverb out of context, as in a list of proverbs. There is no explicit discourse situation to indicate the target domain. Nonetheless we are not inclined to take the statement as purely a description of a storm, because we already know that proverbs concern general issues about the nature of our being, the nature of people and situations we encounter, and our role in the universe. Thus we know from the statement itself that the source domain is storms and from our knowledge about proverbs that the target domain is somehow tightly connected with human concerns.

How do we arrive at a mapping between storms and human affairs? What direction are we given by the statement itself? What do we bring to bear on that statement? The answer has two parts:
— The specific level schema evoked by the words "Big thunder / little rain."
— The GREAT CHAIN METAPHOR.

The GREAT CHAIN METAPHOR applies to the specific-level schema evoked by the words in the following way:
— The Great Chain links storms with human beings.
— The commonsense theory of the Nature of Things picks out attributes and their causal relation to behavior at the levels of storms and human beings.
— The Maxim of Quantity picks out the highest attributes and behavior relevant at each level.
— The GENERIC IS SPECIFIC metaphor extracts from this specific-level knowledge about storms the corresponding generic-level structure. It maps this structure onto the target domain of human beings, picking out the highest level human attributes and behavior which preserves the generic-level structure.

Let us now turn to the details of how this works.

Let us start out by considering how much and what kind of commonplace knowledge about the source domain of storms we bring to bear in understanding this proverb. It is knowledge from the specific-level schema, which contains a broad range of information. For instance, we know that rain is water, that it comes down from the sky, that water is wet, that people out in a storm get wet, and so on. Such knowledge is factored out as irrelevant by the Great Chain + the Nature of Things + the Maxim of Quantity.

It is done in the following way. First, there is what is overtly mentioned in the proverb, namely, the relative amounts of thunder and rain. Next, the commonsense theory of the Nature of Things focuses on the *causal* relation between the thunder and the rain. In terms of Great Chain organization, this causal relation is at a certain level, the level of overall part-whole functional configuration. Since the Maxim of Quantity is applying to the linear scale defined by the Great Chain, it picks out information only at the level of overall functional organization. Lower-level information, such as the fact that rain is made up of water, which is wet, is ruled out as irrelevant. The Maxim of Quantity picks out only the highest level on the grounds that if lower-level information were to be the principal basis for a metaphorical mapping, then the lower-level information would be mentioned in the proverb. Thus, the Great Chain + the Nature of Things + the Maxim of Quantity, applied together, lead us to pick out certain parts of our knowledge about thunderstorms, namely, the overall causal relationship between thunder and rain within the thunderstorm schema:

— A thunderstorm contains (at least) two kinds of causally related natural events within it: the thunder and the rainstorm.
— The thunder precedes and accompanies the rain.
— Before any occurrence of rain, at least one occurrence of thunder communicates to us that the rain will occur.
— Typically, the magnitude of the thunder indicates the magnitude of the rainstorm.

We use this knowledge to understand the expression, "Big thunder / little rain," as referring to an unusual case: although there is a lot of thunder, surprisingly little rain follows; the storm had much less power to affect us than one would expect from the thunder. "Big thunder / little rain"

thus adds to the relevant aspects of thunderstorm schema the following information about the case at hand:
— In this case, the force of the rain is much less than we would expect given the force of the thunder.

Thus far, only the nonmetaphoric aspects of the GREAT CHAIN METAPHOR have been considered, those that pick out the relevant parts of the evoked source-domain schema. The metaphorical work is done by the GENERIC IS SPECIFIC metaphor + the Great Chain. Given the relevant specific-level understanding of "Big thunder / little rain," the GENERIC IS SPECIFIC metaphor picks out the generic-level information it contains. This information is at a certain level in the Great Chain, the level of natural physical events. The following is the generic-level information relevant to our understanding of "Big thunder / little rain," with the restrictions to the domain of natural physical events placed in parentheses:
— There is a (natural physical occurrence) that contains at least two causally related kinds of (natural events) within it.
— The first precedes and accompanies the second.
— Before any (natural event) of the second kind, at least one (natural event) of the first kind communicates to us that the second kind will occur.
— The second has the power to affect us.
— Typically, the magnitude of the first indicates the magnitude of the second.
— In this case, the force of the second is much less than we would expect given the magnitude of the first.

It is the source-domain information with this generic-level structure to which we apply the metaphorical mapping of GREAT CHAIN METAPHOR. The mapping is accomplished through a combination of GENERIC IS SPECIFIC + the Great Chain. What the mapping does is to associate the relevant source-domain information about storms with relevant target-domain information about people. The Great Chain links natural occurrences to human behaviors, and the GENERIC IS SPECIFIC metaphor, in concert with the Great Chain, maps the above generic-level information about natural occurences into the the corresponding generic-level information about human behavior:

— There is a (human behavioral sequence) that contains at least two causally related kinds of (human actions) within it.
— The first precedes and accompanies the second.
— Before any (human action) of the second kind, at least one (human action) of the first kind communicates to us that the second kind will occur.
— The second has the power to affect us.
— Typically, the magnitude of the first indicates the magnitude of the second.
— In this case, the force of the second is much less than we would expect given the magnitude of the first.

This generic-level structure fits what we know about, say, ineffectual bragging. The action of the first kind is an announcement that one's powers are great, as a preparation or warning. The second kind of action is a display of those powers. In ineffectual bragging, the powers displayed are much less than the announcement would warrant.

We have just shown how the parts of the GREAT CHAIN METAPHOR work in concert, much as one might analyze a symphony by picking out the contributions of strings, woodwinds, brass, and tympani. But despite the internal complexity of the GREAT CHAIN METAPHOR, the overall effect seems simple: we can understand "Big thunder / little rain" immediately and with little or no effort as characterizing, say, ineffectual bragging when the proverb is taken in isolation.

This characterization of the GREAT CHAIN METAPHOR has great explanatory power. It explains, for example, why "Big thunder / little rain" cannot mean just anything at all— why, for example, it cannot mean that people love their children, or that red wine goes with meat, or that you just scratched your nose. The explanation involves the evocation of the thunderstorm schema, the choice of which aspects of the schema are relevant, the picking out of the generic-level structure of those aspects of the schema, and the preservation of that structure in a mapping constrained by the Great Chain.

The explanation also predicts that "Big thunder / little rain" can be used to characterize more than just ineffectual bragging. In a different context, there might be a different mapping that picks out the same aspects of the thunderstorm schema, preserves generic-level structure, and is also constrained by the Great Chain. Indeed, it might not even be applied to human beings. For example, "Big thunder / little rain" might be applied to a viciously barking dog, as way of saying that there's no reason to be afraid of him. Such a situation would have the same generic-level structure as was given above, with animal behavior in place of human behavior.

One subtlety of the way the GREAT CHAIN METAPHOR works is worth noting. The cultural model of the Great Chain primarily concerns attributes and behavior; it relates different forms of being only via levels of attributes and behavior. Within the GREAT CHAIN METAPHOR, the Great Chain is used in two ways:

— It can link levels of forms of being, such as natural events and human behavior. In this way it extends the powers of the GENERIC IS SPECIFIC metaphor so that it can allow one level of being to be understood in terms of another.

— The Great Chain model is used in concert with the Maxim of Quantity to pick out the highest relevant level of attributes and behavior within a source-domain schema. The effect is to pick those aspects of the schema that are relevant to metaphorical understanding.

The latter function of the Great Chain model is independent of what the target domain is. Thus, the GREAT CHAIN METAPHOR can apply to a target domain *at the same level* on the Great Chain as the source domain. This does not mean that the Great Chain is not being used. It is still being used, together with the Maxim of Quantity, to pick out the relevant parts of the source domain schema. As an example of this, imagine a situation in which an earthquake has just made a large rumbling noise, and someone says "Big thunder / little rain" to indicate that that the earthquake won't cause much damage. The earthquake domain is at the level of natural physical phenomena, as is the source domain of thunderstorms. But the conceptual complex of the GREAT CHAIN METAPHOR still applies in essentially the same way.

The account we have given also explains why two different proverbs can be used to essentially the same effect. "Big thunder / little rain" works in pretty much the same way as the English proverb "All bark and no bite." The latter proverb evokes our commonplace knowledge about dogs. The GREAT CHAIN METAPHOR applies to this to pick out essentially the same generic-level structure that is picked out in "Big thunder / little rain." For this reason, it can be applied metaphorically to pretty much the same range of cases. The only difference is "All bark and no bite" cannot be applied metaphorically to dogs, but it can be applied metaphorically to thunderstorms.

It should be clear by now that a given proverb can be comprehended in different ways by different mechanisms. For example, in our discussion above of GENERIC IS SPECIFIC, we discussed the following proverbs:

> Blind
> blames the ditch
>
> Burned lips on broth
> now blows on cold water.

We explained that in "Blind / blames the ditch" a certain specific-level schema characterizing a particular incapacity (blindness) included the structure of a generic-level schema of incapacity in general. We also explained that in "Burned lips on broth / now blows on cold water," a certain specific-level schema of a particular traumatic experience (burning) and its particular consequences for habitual behavior (blowing) incorporated a generic-level schema of general traumatic experiences and general consequences for habitual behavior.

These are understandings that we arrived at by virtue of the GENERIC IS SPECIFIC metaphor. But of course we can additionally use the rest of the conceptual complex of the GREAT CHAIN METAPHOR, along with GENERIC IS SPECIFIC, to understand these proverbs. We may understand that higher-order incapacities (such as mental incapacities, like prejudice, ignorance, failure to understand, and so on) are to be understood in terms of the lower-order incapacity of physical perceptual blindness. And we may understand that higher-order trauma and habit (such as a painful emotional experience and consequent habitual ways of dealing with emotional relationships) are to be understood in terms of the lower-order physical trauma of being burned and the lower-order physical habit of blowing on food. These would be interpretations using the GREAT CHAIN METAPHOR.

Now that we have characterized the internal operation of the GREAT CHAIN METAPHOR, we will treat it from here on out as a unitary operation and discuss its internal structure only when necessary.

Exhortation versus Description

So far we have looked at ways proverbs describe. For example, under the interpretation we have given of "Burned lips on broth / now blows on cold water," it could describe a person who has had a painful emotional experience and who now is extremely careful about even minimal emotional involvement.

But proverbs are also used to exhort people to do better. If we take the "Burned lips" proverb as an exhortation, then we conclude that the response *described* must be inadequate, for if it were adequate, the proverb could not be exhorting us to do *better* than that response. What exactly is the proverb exhorting us to do?

Blowing not only on steaming hot water but on cold water as well is an automatic, conditioned, unthinking behavior; that is, it is a lower-order behavior, appropriate only to a conditioned animal, not to a higher-order rational being. The proverb is telling us that we have a choice: instead of using lower-order instinctual behavior, we ought to be engaging in higher-order rational behavior, using rational judgment and choice. We ought to be judging each situation on its merits, not reacting to every situation uniformly.

Exactly how does exhortation work in proverbs? In "Burned lips on broth / now blows on cold water," the proverb exhorts *not* to engage in the behavior described in the proverb. But in "Cows run with the wind / horses against it," the proverb tells us to act like horses, not like cows. That is, it includes two descriptions and exhorts us to act like one and not like the other. How does it accomplish this? And in "Knife / can't whittle its own handle," the proverb does no exhorting at all.

The mechanism for all of this becomes clear when we think about what an exhortation is. An exhortation is, by nature, *a directive to exercise voluntary control*. Exercising voluntary control is a higher-order rational behavior of human beings. The content of the exhortation is given by the metaphorical interpretation of the proverb, which is in the form of a description. The content of the description, whenever possible, is an exhortation to do, or not do, what is metaphorically characterized by the proverb. If the metaphorical description is consistent with voluntary control, then the proverb exhorts us to behave as described; if it is not consistent with voluntary control, then the proverb exhorts us not to behave as the proverb describes. In short, proverbs exhort us to exert voluntary control with respect to the behavior described metaphorically by the proverb.

The opposite of exercising voluntary control is rigid behavior, behavior of the sort described in the "Burned lips" proverb. According to our cultural models, only human beings are capable of exercising voluntary control; all "lower" forms of being behave rigidly. Thus, higher animals act by instinct or conditioning, lower animals and plants by biological laws, and physical objects by physical laws. At lower levels on the Great Chain, the causal relationship between attributes and behavior is a rigid one. Since causal relations are part of generic-level structure, they are preserved by the applications of the GREAT CHAIN METAPHOR. If they are rigid in nature, their rigidity is accordingly preserved. Thus, when we use the GREAT CHAIN METAPHOR to interpret proverbs about lower-order forms of being as being about people, we map over the rigidity of lower-order causal links governing behavior. In such cases, the proverbs, in exhorting us to exert voluntary control, can only be exhorting us *not* to act in accord with the behavior the proverb describes.

Incidentally, exhortation readings are always accompanied by description readings, but not conversely. An exhortation reading *adds* something to the content given by the description. The exhortation is thus dependent on the content of the description, while the description is independent of the exhortation.

As we would expect, given this account, there are times when the exhortation reading is absent, as, for example, with "Knife / can't whittle its own handle." It is absent because the descriptive reading characterizes an essential, unchangeable attribute: the inability to shape one's own character. An exhortation reading of this would be exhorting one to change what is unchangeable, and therefore the reading is impossible.

Of course, in contexts where the description and exhortation readings are both possible, the two readings, while distinct, can both occur simultaneously. That is, "Burned lips on broth / now blows on cold water" could, in a given situation, be used both to describe a particular person and to exhort the addressee not to behave like that person.

Let us now look at further cases illuminating the distinction between exhortation and description:

Cow parched by sun
pants at the moon.

A descriptive reading of this proverb arises from the same mechanism we saw at work in "Burned lips on broth." The GREAT CHAIN METAPHOR allows us to use the lower-order behavior of the source domain, namely, a conditioned physical reflex that results from a traumatic physical experience, to understand a higher-order behavior, one having to do, for instance, with emotions. Because it embodies GENERIC IS SPECIFIC, the GREAT CHAIN METAPHOR allows us to generalize, say, from some particular emotional behavior of this sort to other emotional behaviors of the same sort.

Whereas human beings can make rational judgments and choices, our commonplace notion of cows is that, as creatures of instinct, they lack such powers of judgment and choice. Their behavior is thus rigid. Since rigidity of behavior is a generic-level characteristic, it is preserved by the application of the generic-level GREAT CHAIN METAPHOR in the description reading. The result is a description reading in which "Cow parched by the sun / now pants at the moon" could, like "Burned lips on broth," be used to describe a person who has had a painful emotional experience and now avoids even safe emotional involvements. Of course, on the exhortation reading, we are exhorted to exercise voluntary control and, hence, not to act like the cow.

Consider another case:

Frog
forgets he had a tail

At the specific level, we know that frogs develop from tadpoles, which have tails, and we assume that frogs cannot remember their earlier stage of life as tadpoles. Contained in this specific-level knowledge is the generic-level knowledge that the animal mentioned cannot remember the stages of life that led to its present existence. Part of our cultural model of animals is that animals, including frogs, function in the present without an awareness of their past. Since they have no choice in the matter, this is a form of rigid behavior. Therefore, to describe a person by "Frog / forgets he had a tail" is to attribute to that person a rigidity of behavior: functioning without an awareness of one's origins. As an exhortation, "Frog / forgets he had a tail" exhorts us not to behave in this way, but rather to remember our origins.

Consider a last example:

Charcoal
writes everybody's name
black

This can be understood as a description of someone who slanders others indiscriminately and uncontrollably, not because the victims of the slander deserve it, but rather because the person is inherently malicious.

This interpretation arises in this way. Charcoal is a physical substance. By its very nature, it is black all the way through and the blackness rubs off on anything it touches. It is a consequence of the inherent nature of charcoal that any mark it makes is black. In this sense, the behavior of charcoal is rigid; charcoal can't help but make anything it touches black.

The proverb makes use of the conventional metaphor that BAD IS BLACK, the conventional metonymy that NAME STANDS FOR REPUTATION, and the knowledge that writing is communication at the generic level. Applying the GREAT CHAIN METAPHOR, we get the following mapping:

— Charcoal, inherently black throughout, maps onto a person inherently bad throughout. Hence, human character is being understood in terms of physical nature.

— Writing someone's name black maps onto slandering that person, that is, communicating that he or she has a bad reputation.

In addition, the rigidity of the causal link between what charcoal is like and what it does is preserved in the mapping, because it is a generic-level attribute. This yields the interpretation that the slanderer can't help slandering any more than the charcoal can help writing black. Thus, the victims of the slander are not suspect; the slanderer is.

This proverb *could* also be used to exhort, though the situation would have to be unusual. The resulting exhortation would be to exercise what voluntary control we have over our own character so as to control what is bad in it. We should not remain fixed in our character as the charcoal is fixed in its blackness: we should use our judgment and not say bad things about people unthinkingly and indiscriminately.

Interactions with Basic Metaphors

In arriving at an understanding of "Charcoal / writes everybody's name / black," we make use of the conventional metonymy NAME STANDS FOR REPUTATION and the conventional metaphor GOOD IS WHITE; BAD IS BLACK, which underlie the expression, "to blacken someone's name." Such interaction of conventional metaphors and metonymies with generic-level metaphors occurs frequently.

Suppose, for example, we interpret "Frog / forgets he had a tail," as describing a high official who acts as if he earned his rank on his own, when in fact his family made sacrifices to educate and raise him so that he could attain such a position.

Why tail? How can we understand that *tail* maps onto

one's past, in this case, one's family heritage? The mapping involves complex interactions, as follows. The major work is done by the GREAT CHAIN METAPHOR, which allows us to understand human nature in terms of animal instinctual and biological nature. In doing so, the GREAT CHAIN META-PHOR must preserve generic-level information in the target domain, except for what the metaphor itself changes. But this preservation, in this case, relies on the following assistance. We have a metaphoric understanding of our past as "part" of us, and another metaphoric understanding that a person moves forward through time toward the future, "leaving his past behind him," so that what is physically behind corresponds to what is temporally past. Thus, by virtue of these metaphoric understandings, it is possible to map a part of an animal that is physically behind onto a person's past—a "part" that is temporally "behind" him—and still preserve generic-level structure. With this assistance, the GREAT CHAIN METAPHOR can map the lower-order animal behavior onto the higher-order human behavior. That lower-order animal behavior is, at its generic level: an animal had a tail, a hind part, functionally dominant and developmentally indispensable, but the animal is no longer aware it had the part. Via the GREAT CHAIN METAPHOR, this maps onto: a person has a past that is "part" of him, that is temporally behind him, and that once was functionally dominant and indispensable to his development, but he has now forgotten that he had such a past.

Let us now take up the full details of a more extended example of metaphorical interaction. Consider:

Jelly
in a vise

Until now, we have mostly given only one reading of any proverb, although we have been careful to speak of "possible readings" and to point out that readings of proverbs vary with context. We would now like to take up some examples of very different readings of a single proverb, "Jelly / in a vise," to show how the mechanisms we have been describing can characterize whole ranges of readings, even readings with opposite values and intents. What we will find is that proverbs are always understood relative to a background of assumptions and values, and with different backgrounds the same metaphor can lead to very different interpretations.

This proverb presents a vivid, concrete image of a source domain, with no mention of the target domain of human affairs. We take the target domain to be human affairs, either because the discourse situation indicates it or because we know that proverbs typically concern human affairs. Let us begin with readings in which the GREAT CHAIN META-PHOR applies to the jelly, interpreting it as a person.

In the first reading we will consider, the jelly refers to a person who has the characteristic capacity to be flexible in confrontational, competitive, and antagonistic situations. Such a person, by virtue of his or her flexibility, has many dimensions of freedom and is therefore not easily boxed in. In this reading, the person referred to as jelly might be described as having a genius for supple behavior under pressure, as talented at getting out of tight spots.

In another, supplementary reading, the GREAT CHAIN METAPHOR also maps the vise onto a person—one who is trying to dominate something, to bind it, incapacitate it, tie it down, but whose powers are very limited in their range and no match for the powers of what he or she wants to dominate. These readings can reinforce each other: one person (the vise) may be using flat-footed and inappropriate powers to dominate some other person (the jelly) who has the capacity to escape those powers.

In this combined reading, the target domain concerns characteristic behaviors of people as they derive from essential character attributes; this is understood in terms of a source domain of physical events caused by essential physical attributes. The physical slippage of the jelly is mapped onto the metaphoric slippage of the wily person; the physical horizontal clamping of the vise is mapped onto the metaphoric one-dimensional clamping of the person who wishes to dominate. The essential physical slipperiness of the jelly is mapped onto the character of the wily person, who is characteristically "slippery." The essential physical hardness, rigidity, and one-dimensional clamping of the vise are mapped onto the character of the person who wishes to dominate, who is characteristically powerful and capable of bearing down, but inflexible in direction.

This reading is based on a background schema in which there is a competitive situation in which avoiding domination is the main goal and avoiding confrontation is a virtue. The jelly wins just by being itself with no effort, while the vise exhausts itself to no end. The jelly is therefore viewed positively, and such a slippery person can be spoken of in positive terms as "wily." In this sense, a guerrilla army confronted by a conventional army might be viewed as "Jelly / in a vise."

On this reading the jelly has won. Let us now consider a second reading, again in a competitive situation. This time, confrontation is considered to be a virtue—standing up and fighting to retain one's integrity. Here the vise has won, the jelly having lost all integrity. The victor might say, "We squashed 'em just like jelly in a vise."

Here we have the GREAT CHAIN METAPHOR applying in different ways—even with the same background schema of antagonistic competition. The difference in the readings comes from different construals of what counts as winning.

Let us now turn to a third reading, one which is framed not in terms of antagonistic competition but rather in terms of social interaction. Assume a situation in which what is valued is stability and social "contact." Then "slipperiness" is antisocial behavior detrimental to everyone. Here the focus is not on the forcefulness of the vise that, but rather the fact that a vise is a useful, indeed necessary tool for holding objects in place so that one can interact productively with them. Again, the vise is mapped onto a person, this time seen positively as a promoter of stability and social contact. THE GREAT CHAIN METAPHOR is again applied, with a different framing of the situation to yield very different results: whenever the vise tries to make contact and establish a personal interaction with some solidity, the jelly squirms out of it, by nature incapable of solid interpersonal relationships, someone you would not want to try to interact with and who could not be counted on to be there when needed.

Now let us turn to a fourth, and quite different, reading—one in which there is a delicate, somewhat sticky situation to be dealt with, which will become messy if not handled with great care. Here the jelly is the delicate situation. There is a person who has to deal with it, but one who has no sense of delicacy at all. The only tool this person has for dealing with the world is the vise, which is completely inappropriate and makes a mess of the situation. In this case, the GREAT CHAIN METAPHOR applies in a very different way, mapping physical properties, goals, means, and behavior onto higher-order properties, goals, means, and behavior.

From these examples, it is clear that proverbs can have an enormous range of readings, depending on the framings one brings to them. But this does not mean that readings are arbitrary and that just any reading is possible. All these readings are guided by a single generic-level metaphor, the GREAT CHAIN METAPHOR, and all the readings based on that metaphor, though there are many possibilities, will be readings in which attributes and behaviors higher in the Great Chain are understood in terms of attributes and behaviors lower on the Chain.

Let us now return to the lines from Yeats we quoted at the beginning of this chapter as an example of how our most famous poets constantly use the mechanisms of metaphor we find in anonymous proverbial poetry:

> Cast a cold eye
> On life, on death.
> Horseman, pass by!

Here we have a gravestone and a horseman, who, reading the inscription, is given an instruction by the person whose grave it is. "On life, on death" and "horseman" together evoke the LIFE IS A JOURNEY metaphor. This metaphor maps the horseman, a robust and adventuresome person, onto a robust person in mid life, and his encounter with the tombstone onto a significant event in life. The grave, which the horseman encounters in midjourney, marks the end of the speaker's life journey.

"Cast a cold eye" is metaphorically complex. "Cold" is metaphorically dispassionate, as in "cool reason." The basic

189

metaphor is PASSIONATE IS HOT; DISPASSIONATE IS COLD. "Cast an eye" makes use of two basic metaphors: First, there is SEEING IS TOUCHING, as in "lay eyes on" and "can't take my eyes off," in which vision is understood in terms of a "line of sight" reaching out from the eye and resting on what is seen. Second, KNOWING IS SEEING maps what is seen onto what is known. "Casting an eye," which is active looking, thus maps onto an active understanding of the scene, which, with "cold" added, yields an active, dispassionate understanding of the scene. Thus, "cast a cold eye" is an instruction to observe the tombstone and dispassionately assess its significance.

The source-domain instruction to the horseman is to observe the scene of the tombstone, which is on his journey, and to continue the journey. Putting all these basic metaphors together, we get a metaphorical instruction to assess dispassionately this event in life and to go on with one's life.

This is as far as the basic, specific-level metaphors take us in the reading. None of these specific-level metaphors tells us anything about the relationship between Yeats's life and the life of the person reading the tombstone. For example, the LIFE IS A JOURNEY metaphor makes no mention of how one is to comprehend the death of another person. The specific-level metaphors involved do not tell us what the significance of the encounter is.

The ultimate moral of the inscription on the tombstone is this: Yeats's grave has a different significance for him than it does for us. Yeats has come to the end of his life and is in his natural and appropriate resting place in the Irish countryside under Ben Bulben. But we are still alive; for us this is only a stopping point; we have the rest of our lives to live in whatever ways are appropriate for us. We should live our lives in the rational awareness that each life is different and that dwelling too long over the passing of others only diverts one from one's own life adventure.

Here is how the GREAT CHAIN METAPHOR, together with the other metaphors, yields this reading. First, start with two lives, Yeats's and the horseman's, both understood as journeys. The physical journeys intersect at Yeats's grave: it is the endpoint of his and a midpoint on the horseman's.

LIFE IS A JOURNEY does not map such an intersection. But, given the other two mappings, the GREAT CHAIN META-PHOR can complete the job, mapping the lower-order physical relationship between the journeys onto a higher-order "philosophical" relationship between the lives.

Next, take the horseman's physical observation of the scene of the grave, which, as we saw, maps onto a dispassionate assessment of that scene. Since that scene is the intersection of the two physical journeys, the GREAT CHAIN METAPHOR maps it onto the dispassionate assessment of the intersection of the two lives: the end of one is the middle of the other.

Now recall that we have a sequence of directives: cast a cold eye . . . pass by. Such a sequence is typically understood as: Do the first; if you do the first, then you will do the second. An example might be "Be reasonable. Give up." Our use of all the basic metaphors plus the GREAT CHAIN METAPHOR yields the following interpretation of the sequences of directives: First, dispassionately assess the relationship between the two lives: the end of one is the midpoint of the other. Now, if you have dispassionately assessed the situation, you will go on with your life.

We see in these three lines by Yeats the same kinds of interaction we have seen throughout the proverbs discussed in this section. In particular, the generic-level GREAT CHAIN METAPHOR interacts with four basic metaphors: LIFE IS A JOURNEY, KNOWING IS SEEING, SEEING IS TOUCHING, and DISPASSIONATE IS COLD.

Social and Psychological Forces

We normally think of force as something physical. A vise is a tool that allows one to exert a physical force on physical objects. When we understand "Jelly / in a vise" metaphorically in terms of the GREAT CHAIN METAPHOR, we understand the physical force exerted by the vise as mapping onto forces at higher levels—social, psychological, emotional, and intellectual forces. For example, competition can occur in any of these domains, and therefore a slippery person can avoid forces of all of these kinds. Similarly, the English proverb "If you don't bend, you break" has as its source domain physical objects and the physical forces applying to them. the GREAT CHAIN METAPHOR allows a wide variety of interpretations of this proverb in which the forces involved can be either social, psychological, emotional, or intellectual. As one example, we might interpret this proverb as giving advice to a scientific theorist about how to construct his theories: they must be sufficiently flexible so that, when the force of reason is applied to them, they will be able to bend, that is, adjust a little, instead of breaking, that is, being destroyed.

Natural forces are special cases of physical forces, and they too can be interpreted in this way using the GREAT CHAIN METAPHOR. Consider:

> Cows run with the wind
> horses against it.

Here, the wind is a natural force, and cows and horses, having different instinctual natures, behave differently in response to that natural force. Metaphorically, the natural force of the wind can be understood as, say, a kind of social or psychological force, and the cows and horses as two different sorts of people who have different essential characters, and hence different characteristic behaviors in response to those metaphoric forces.

Contingent Attributes and Behavior

The GREAT CHAIN METAPHOR operates over contingent as well as essential attributes and behavior. Consider the English proverb, "Strike while the iron is hot." One of the physical properties of iron is that it is temporarily malleable when heated. Therefore, if a blacksmith wishes to change the shape of a piece of iron, the most effective course he can take is to "strike while the iron is hot," since it will take much more effort to change the shape of the iron after it cools off—if it can be done at all.

Heat is, for most things, a contingent physical property. Metaphorically, it can map onto contingent higher-order properties, such as, for example, sexual arousal. Here, the GREAT CHAIN METAPHOR can map the iron onto a person who is sexually aroused and the blacksmith onto a person who is trying to seduce that person (that is, to effect a considerable change in the shape of their relationship). "Strike while the iron is hot" can therefore be interpreted as advice that seduction is most likely to succeed when the person to be seduced is sexually aroused.

Contingent human attributes can also be understood in terms of contingent animal attributes. Consider the proverb "Let sleeping dogs lie." Here we are understanding mental inattentiveness in terms of the biological process of sleep. We know that someone who is sleeping cannot interfere with us. This knowledge is brought to bear on our understanding of this proverb. In addition, we know that dogs that are awake can be threatening or bothersome, while dogs that are asleep are not. Thus, their temporary attributes (being asleep or not) lead to their contingent behavior (being threatening or bothersome, or not).

The GREAT CHAIN METAPHOR allows us to understand this proverb as applying to people who are mentally inattentive to what we are doing. It says that they will not be threatening or bothersome as long as we do not do anything that will make them more attentive.

Metaphorical schemas

Sometimes we understand people in terms of animals or other lower-order forms of being. Sometimes we understand those lower-order forms of being in terms of people. For example, we can understand wines as having a character, as being, say, "unpretentious"; desserts as being, "seductive"; perfumes as being, perhaps, "bold" or "playful"; and so on.

One of the most elaborate domains in which we understand the nonhuman in terms of the human is the domain of animal life. There we have well-elaborated schemas characterizing what animals are like, and we usually understand their characteristics metaphorically in terms of the characteristics of human beings. Here are some common propositions that occur in schemas for animals:

— Pigs are dirty, messy, and rude.

— Lions are courageous and noble.
— Foxes are clever.
— Dogs are loyal, dependable, and dependent.
— Cats are fickle and independent.
— Wolves are cruel and murderous.
— Gorillas are aggressive and violent.

These are *metaphorical* propositions within schemas. They all involve conventionalized instances of the GREAT CHAIN METAPHOR, through which properties of things lower on the chain are understood in terms of human properties. Our folk understandings of what these animals are like is metaphorical. We understand their attributes in terms of *human* character traits. We think of them, react to them, and treat them as we would a person with such traits.

Animals act instinctively, and different kinds of animals have different kinds of instinctive behavior. We comprehend their behavior in terms of human behavior, and we use the language of human character traits to describe such behavior. Cleverness, loyalty, courage, rudeness, dependability, and fickleness are *human* character traits, and when we attribute such character traits to animals we are comprehending the behavior of those animals metaphorically in human terms.

It is so natural for us to understand nonhuman attributes in terms of our own human character traits that we often have difficulty realizing that such characterizations of animals are metaphorical. Take the loyalty we attribute to dogs and the courage we attribute to lions. Human loyalty requires a moral sense and a capacity for reflective moral judgment. Human courage requires an awareness of danger, a moral judgment that places the importance of the act above the danger, and a conscious will to carry out the act under those circumstances. We know that dogs lack a moral sense and a capacity for moral judgment. And we know that lions too lack moral judgment and the capacity to weigh personal danger against moral correctness. Dogs and lions behave the way they do out of instinct, but we commonly understand their behavior as if it were the product of some character trait of a human being.

Some Classic Examples

We are now in a position to discuss an important class of examples, a class that has come up repeatedly in the history of theorizing about metaphor. These are cases like "Achilles is a lion," "Man is a wolf," and so on. The most usual cases are of the form "A is a B," where B is a concept characterized by a metaphorical schema of the sort we have just discussed.

Let us take "Achilles is a lion" as a typical case. In our schema for "lion," certain of a lion's instinctive traits are understood metaphorically in terms of human character traits, such as courage.

— The expression "Achilles is a lion" invites us to understand the character of Achilles in terms of a certain instinctive trait of lions, a trait which is already *metaphorically understood in terms of a character trait of humans*. There is a boring part and two interesting parts in this process. The boring part is that we understand the characteristic courage of Achilles in terms of something that is already metaphorically understood in terms of the human trait of courage: this is equivalent to calling Achilles courageous.

The first interesting part is understanding the *character* of Achilles in terms of the *instinct* of the lion: this asks us to understand the steadfastness of Achilles' courage in terms of the rigidity of animal instinct. Achilles' courage, we are to understand, is as unchanging and reliable as if it were an animal instinct. The mechanism by which this works is the GREAT CHAIN METAPHOR: steadfastness of higher-order character is understood in terms of rigidity of lower-order instinct. Thus the first interesting part of the metaphor is not that Achilles is being characterized as courageous but that the steadfastness of his courage is characterized as being as rigid as the instinctual behavior of an animal.

What is boring about the boring part is not that there is no metaphor being employed. Instead, there are *two*: they go in opposite directions and they cancel each other out. First, independent of the metaphor involving Achilles and the lion, the metaphorical schema evoked by the word "lion" makes use of a conventionalized instance of the

GREAT CHAIN METAPHOR, through which we understand nonhuman attributes in terms of human character traits. We thus begin with a conventional understanding of a certain behavior of the lion in terms of the courageous behavior of a human.

Second, the expression "Achilles is a lion" makes use of the GREAT CHAIN METAPHOR going in the opposite direction, inviting us to understand human behavior in terms of animal behavior. Specifically, the human character trait of courage is first metaphorically mapped onto the conventional schema for lion to create our commonplace schema of a lion. Then, in "Achilles is a lion," we are invited to map that human character trait back onto a human, Achilles. The two processes are converses of one another, which is why they cancel each other out. This is why it seems plausible to say that "Achilles is a lion" does no more than say that Achilles is courageous.

Of course, as we have seen, there is real metaphorical work going on here that is not canceled out, namely, understanding the *steadfastness* of Achilles' courage in terms of the *rigidity* of the lion's animal instinct. This real metaphoric work concerns not the properties in the source and target schemas but rather the structures of those schemas. In the lion schema, the property of "courage" stands in a certain relation to the lion: it is a *rigid* property because it is instinctual. When we understand Achilles in terms of a lion, we map the lion onto Achilles, the lion's "courage" onto Achilles's courage, and *the relation between the lion and his "courage" onto the relation between Achilles and his courage.*

The second interesting part in the mapping also concerns mapping the structure of the source schema onto the target schema. We often conceive of things as having quintessential properties: we can say that piety is the quintessential characteristic of the saint, that filthiness is the quintessential characteristic of pigs, and that courage is the quintessential characteristic of lions. In our schema for lion, the property of courage is marked as being a special property for the lion: it is its quintessential characteristic. This relation between the lion and his "courage" is also mapped onto the schema for Achilles: courage becomes the quintessential characteristic of Achilles.

To clarify what is involved in mapping the structure of a schema as opposed to properties in that schema, let us consider the sentence "Heather's a time bomb," where the correspondence is determined by an independently existing metaphor. "Heather's a time bomb" would usually be understood via our conventional way of understanding anger metaphorically, in which suddenly getting violently angry is "exploding." Thus, we understand "Heather's a time bomb" via the following mechanisms:

— The quintessential characteristic of a time bomb is: it is going to explode, but we (the potential victims) do not know just when.

— This has the generic-level structure of: it is going to do something sudden and forceful, but we don't know just when.

— The anger metaphor maps "Heather's a time bomb" into: Heather is suddenly going to get violently angry, but we do not know just when.

— The anger metaphor thus establishes an independent connection between exploding and suddenly getting violently angry.

— Given this connection, the GREAT CHAIN METAPHOR can apply to that property, exploding suddenly, together with its generic-level structure, which includes the specification that it is a *quintessential* property.

— Since the GREAT CHAIN METAPHOR is a generic-level metaphor, and since the *quintessential* nature of a property is part of generic-level structure, the GREAT CHAIN METAPHOR maps over the *quintessential* nature of the property.

— Thus, the GREAT CHAIN METAPHOR, forming a composite with the anger metaphor, attributes to Heather the complex property: "will suddenly get violently angry, but it is not known when." In addition, it assigns this property to Heather as a *quintessential* characteristic.

Thus, the GREAT CHAIN METAPHOR can have subtle but important effects. Because it preserves generic-level structure, and because rigidity and quintessentiality are part of generic-level structure, they can be mapped over by the GREAT CHAIN METAPHOR. Because rigidity and quintessentiality are not attributes of objects but rather attributes of attributes, they are often overlooked despite their importance.

The Similarity Theory

Cases like "Achilles is a lion" have given rise to a false general theory of metaphor, the similarity theory, which claims that metaphor consists in the highlighting of similarities. Metaphorical expressions like "Achilles is a lion" are commonly taken to be support for the similarity theory on these grounds: the sentence maintains that Achilles is similar to a lion with respect to what we take to be a property of the lion, its "courage." For this argument to work, the "courage" of the lion would have to be "the same literal property" as the "courage" of Achilles. But we have claimed that, literally, lions do not have human courage; they have an instinctive behavior that we understand metaphorically in terms of human courage. The literal similarity that is claimed for the "courage" of Achilles and the lion is actually metaphorical similarity.

But even if one mistakenly believed that the courage of Achilles is the same literal property as the "courage" of the lion, the similarity theory would still fail as an explanation of this example: the courage of Achilles is a property of his *character*, while the courage of the lion is an *instinctual* attribute. Therefore, character is still being understood metaphorically in terms of instinct.

Moreover, the similarity theory fails to account for the mapping of schema structure. The rigidity and quintessential nature of the lion's "courage" are mapped over onto the nature of Achilles' courage, making the courage of Achilles steadfast and quintessential.

For these reasons, "Achilles is a lion" does not provide support for the similarity theory of metaphor, which claims that *all* metaphor rests on preexisting literal similarity. In short, the similarity theory fails even for many of what are supposed to be its strongest cases.

Can Anything Be Anything?

We have shown throughout this chapter that powerful generic-level metaphors enable us to map from varieties of source domains to varieties of target domains. We have shown that they apply to so many different specific-level schemas that one may be tempted to wonder whether there are any restrictions at all on understanding any random schema in terms of any other random schema. In short, can a metaphor exist between any two things?

There is a phenomenon that might make it initially plausible to think that the answer to this question is yes. The phenomenon is that people are very inventive in finding ways of understanding one thing in terms of another. If we give someone two things like "president" and "spider," or like "death" and "magician," can he or she construct a metaphoric understanding that makes sense of "The president is a spider" and "Death is a magician"? Perhaps so. To do this, one would bring to bear a wide range of conceptual machinery—alternative schemas that can be evoked by a given word, extensions of those schemas, alternative cultural background knowledge, assumptions about context, the full range of conventional metaphors and metonymies, and the capacity to form one-shot image-metaphors.

Suppose we call upon our knowledge that the president is a competitive politician who must therefore deal with political enemies. Similarly, we call upon our knowledge of a spider as an insect that lays traps for its prey to stumble into unawares. We can use the GREAT CHAIN METAPHOR to understand the conscious planning behavior of the president in terms of the instinctual predatory behavior of the spider: the president, with stealth and cunning, lays elegant and invisible traps for his political enemies, with the spider's web mapped onto such traps.

Or take "Death is a magician." Suppose we take the normal view of death as the permanent cessation of life and a schema for a magician as someone who makes things disappear. We can then apply EVENTS ARE ACTIONS to map between these selected schemas in such a way as to fit the constraints on that generic-level metaphor. We then arrive at a reading of "Death is a magician" in which death is a personified force that makes living things disappear. Here, EVENTS ARE ACTIONS preserves the generic-level structure of disappearance.

There are, of course, additional possibilities for interpretation. For example, we might take alternative views of both death and magicians, assuming a reincarnation theory of death and viewing the magician as someone who makes things both disappear and return. EVENTS ARE ACTIONS would apply here as before, this time preserving a different generic-level structure, one of disappearance and return.

But this phenomenon—our wide-ranging ability to find ways to metaphorically link two linguistic expressions—does not mean that metaphor is completely unconstrained, that anything can map onto anything any old way. For example, if we understand the event of death metaphorically in terms of the action of a magician, then the general shape of the event must be preserved. The magician causes the disappearance, and therefore, the magician must map onto what causes the death. *Magician* cannot, for example, be mapped onto *the biological expiration of the dying person*. The magician cannot be the dying person's last breath. The magician cannot be the way a terminally ill patient looks. None of these mappings preserves the general shape of the event, including the causal connections. For that reason they are disallowed, by which we mean that they make no ostensible sense to us, and so we dismiss them.

Similarly, if we bring to bear the GREAT CHAIN META-PHOR in order to understand the president in terms of the spider, then our reading must conform to the Maxim of Quantity, which guides us to use the highest-level attributes of the source and target domains unless we are otherwise instructed. We cannot, for example, understand that spiders are black, and black stands for sin, and therefore that "The president is a spider" means that the president is sin, because that reading does not conform to the Maxim of Quantity. It fails to do so because spiders, being lower animals, have as their highest-order properties things like instinctive behavior, not physical properties like color. The

Maxim of Quantity will thus guide us to use the instinctive behavior of the spider and not its color in understanding "The president is a spider."

Though generic-level metaphors permit a wide range of inventive interpretations, those interpretations are by no means arbitrary. They must fit the overall system of constraints imposed by the nature of metaphorical mappings. Consider:

Any weather
chicken's
pants are rolled up

Take one interpretation of this Asian figure. Since this is a proverb, it is about people. Unlike most of the other proverbs we have discussed, the target domain of people is explicitly evoked by the word "pants." The source domain is that of animals, in particular, chickens. The proverb is based on an image-mapping from chickens to people. In Asia, it is common for barefoot peasants working in the fields to roll up their pants when it rains so that they don't get their pants wet when they step into puddles. When they step into muddy puddles, they extend one leg without weight, testing the bottom of the puddle before they put weight on the extended leg. As a result they look as if they are walking stiff legged.

The reading we will consider begins with this conventional image together with the conventional image of a chicken walking. The expression "chicken's / pants" triggers an image-metaphor in which the image of the chicken is mapped onto the image of the peasant, with the chicken's thigh feathers mapped onto the pants, the chicken's legs mapped onto the peasant's legs, and the chicken's walk mapped onto the peasant's stiff-legged walk.

The image-metaphor triggers an application of the GREAT CHAIN METAPHOR, in which the peasant's characteristic behavior is understood in terms of the chicken's characteristic behavior. The chicken, by its nature, has its leg sticking out from its thigh feathers and walks stiff-leggedly. The "any weather" in the proverb suggests that the peasant walks around all the time in the awkward way one is forced to walk after the rain. Via the metaphor that HABITUAL BE-HAVIOR IS AN ATTRIBUTE, the peasant's constant walking around stiff-leggedly with his pants rolled up can be seen as one of his attributes, in this case a character attribute. The GREAT CHAIN METAPHOR links this to the biologically based behavioral attributes of the chicken, providing an understanding of the blind rigidity of the peasant's behavior in terms of the biological necessity of the chicken's. The moral is that the peasant is stupid because he is being inappropriately rigid about something that, as a human being, he can change.

But the proverb, of course, is not about walking around with our pants rolled up. It is about any such awkward and unnecessary habitual behavior. The GENERIC IS SPECIFIC metaphor takes the specific-level behavior of walking around all the time with our pants rolled up and maps it onto the general case: we are stupid if we habitually do something awkward when we do not have to.

This reading is an exhortation not to behave in a certain way. As we saw before, whenever there is an exhortation reading, there is a corresponding description reading. In this case, the description reading is as follows: once you get into the habit of doing something, no matter how awkward, that pattern is as immutable as if it were a biological necessity. Here the proverb describes the peasant as inevitably conditioned to continue doing what he has been doing. The moral here is: Don't think you can change a conditioned behavior.

Such readings, as we would expect, require imaginative construal, and people differ in their abilities to produce such readings. However, that does not mean that imagination is completely free and unconstrained. Consider some of the constraints on these readings. The image-metaphor maps the chicken's legs onto a person's legs. It cannot map the chicken's legs onto something arbitrary, like a person's eyes or a balloon. Furthermore, being generic-level metaphors, GENERIC IS SPECIFIC and the GREAT CHAIN META-PHOR require us to preserve generic-level information.

Thus, one could not come up with just any old reading, such as "Peasants sometimes cook their rice incorrectly" or "People are dangerous when they drink too much."

Though wide-ranging metaphorical interpretations are possible, they are far from arbitrary. A metaphor, after all, is not a linguistic expression. It is a mapping from one conceptual domain to another, and as such it has a three part structure: two endpoints (the source and target schemas) and a bridge between them (the detailed mapping). Such structures are highly constrained. It is not the case that anything can be anything.

The combination of openness to interpretation and strong constraints defines a challenge. Given two phrases that we are to connect metaphorically, the challenge is to find schemas plausibly evoked by those phrases in context, and a bridge of metaphor between them that satisfies the constraints. This is a standard challenge taken up in every avant-garde poetic movement. It was realized perhaps most self-consciously by the surrealists, who formulated it as an artistic principle to challenge the reader to find ways of bringing disparate things together:

> My wife with the sex of a mirror
> My wife with eyes full of tears
> With eyes that are purple armor and a magnetized
>   needle
> With eyes of savannahs
> With eyes full of water to drink in prisons
> My wife with eyes that are forests forever under
>   the ax
> My wife with eyes that are the equal of water
>   and air and earth and fire
> (André Breton, "Free Union," trans. David Antin)

Challenging old ways of understanding the world and bringing readers to experience new ways was a political issue for the surrealists, as it has often been for the avant-garde. The theorists of the avant-garde, in promoting new poetic forms to create new ways of understanding the world, have been acutely aware that classical forms of poetry implicitly embody ideologies—views of man and his relation to nature, to society, and to the cosmos.

Society and the Cosmos

So far, the highest point on the Great Chain that we have mentioned has been the human level. But there are higher levels still—society and, above that at the most embracing level of all, the cosmos. These are metaphorical extensions of the chain, in which the GREAT CHAIN METAPHOR operates not merely to characterize the nature of these levels but in fact to *create* them.

We understand societies as forms of being metaphorically in terms of the forms of being below them on the Great Chain. We speak of a "just society," a "peace-loving nation," and "the evil empire," as if they had the equivalent of human character attributes. We speak of "growth" and "development" of nations, as if they had life cycles. We speak of "satellite countries," as if they were natural objects subject to natural forces.

Societies are also understood as having natural attributes that lead to natural behaviors. They can be understood as aggressive or submissive, intractable or changeable; and how we understand them as behaving depends upon what traits we see them as having. We can understand them in terms of lower-order forms of being via the GREAT CHAIN METAPHOR. In "China is a great sleeping bear—don't awaken her," we are understanding the attributes and behavior of a society in terms of the attributes and behavior of an animal. The mechanism is very much the same as in the interpretation we gave of "Let sleeping dogs lie," though there we were understanding the attributes and behavior of people in terms of those of animals.

The Great Chain is extended to the cosmos in a similar way. The very universe is understood metaphorically as a form of being in terms of lower-order forms of being. We speak of an "indifferent," "benevolent," or "malevolent" universe, as if the universe had human character traits. The universe too is conceived of as having an essential nature which is manifested in the way it operates. This inexorable

operation of the universe is referred to as fate or destiny.
Consider:

> Ants on a millstone
> whichever way they walk
> they go around with it.

In this proverb we are presented with an image of a source
domain, but there is no mention of a target domain. We
know that proverbs are about human affairs, which leads us
to fix a target domain in the upper levels of the Great Chain.
The GREAT CHAIN METAPHOR allows us to provide a reading: the efforts that individual people make to conduct their
lives are relatively insignificant compared to the influence of
the workings of the cosmos on their lives.

In this reading, ants correspond to people, the movement
of the ants to human endeavors, the millstone to the cosmos, the movements of the millstone to the workings of the
cosmos, and, above all, the path along which the millstone
carries the ants corresponds to the result of cosmic influ-
ences on individual human lives.

Exactly how do we arrive at such correspondences? Because we know this is a proverb, it must be about people.
Since the source domain is about ants and a millstone, that
is, lower-order forms of being, and since the target domain
is human affairs, it is natural to bring to bear the GREAT
CHAIN METAPHOR in interpreting this proverb. Because it
is a generic-level metaphor, it will preserve as much as possible of the generic-level relational information in the source
domain, namely:
— The rotating millstone has a fixed circular boundary and
  its motion is internal to that bounded region.
— The ants are contained within that bounded region.
  The motion of the millstone carries the ants with it.
— The ants have an independent self-propelled motion.
— The ants are minuscule relative to the millstone.
— For this reason, the contribution the ants make to the
  path they travel on is insignificant relative to the contri-
  bution made by the motion of the millstone.
— The ants are so small that the millstone constitutes their

entire frame of reference and they cannot perceive its continuous undifferentiated motion.

— Only from a perspective large enough to include the millstone can one perceive the true motion of the ants.

The GREAT CHAIN METAPHOR allows us to map the ants onto people and the millstone onto the cosmos. Thus, people are understood in terms of lower-order insects and the cosmos is understood in terms of a lower-order machine, that is, a physical object with a functional structure.

In understanding the human situation from a cosmic perspective in this proverb, we make use of a number of diverse basic metaphors, in composition with the GREAT CHAIN METAPHOR. First, the path of the ant corresponds to the course of a human life, via LIFE IS A JOURNEY. Therefore, we understand that the individual human's effect on the course of his or her life is insignificant relative to the influence of the workings of the cosmos. What the ant can see of its situation maps onto what a person can know of his or her situation, via KNOWING IS SEEING. The relative sizes of the enormous millstone and the tiny ant map onto the relative importance of the all-important cosmos and the insignificant individual, via IMPORTANT IS BIG.

The choice of ants and a millstone is by no means arbitrary. Relative to human beings, ants and the motions of ants all look alike and what any individual ant does is insignificant. A millstone is an apt source domain for understanding the cosmos because there is an existing conventional metaphor, PERFECT IS REGULAR, that lets us link them naturally. As we saw in chapter three, there is a folk theory of the cosmos in which what is cosmic (or divine) is perfect. A millstone has a regular shape—a circle—and its motion is smooth and regular. Thus, the perfect nature and operation of the cosmos can be understood in terms of the regular shape and motion of the millstone, via PERFECT IS REGULAR.

We now see that the GREAT CHAIN METAPHOR can also be used to understand the cosmos and the human condition within it. In this proverb, it applies twice, mapping the millstone onto the cosmos and the ants onto people. Moreover, the GREAT CHAIN METAPHOR, which is a generic-level metaphor, operates on the generic-level relations in the source schema. For example, it operates on the size relation between the ant and the millstone, requiring that relation to be mapped into some higher-order relation or other at the level of the cosmos, but does not give us the details of the mapping. Relative size is mapped onto relative significance, via the additional, compatible metaphor IMPORTANT IS BIG, which fixes these details. Similarly, the path of the ant through space (resulting from both its own action and that of the millstone) is mapped by the GREAT CHAIN METAPHOR onto something of the same basic shape at the cosmic level. The LIFE IS A JOURNEY metaphor fills in the details of that mapping, picking out the course of life as the target, which is what enables us to understand the proverb as being about the course of human life.

We have just seen that the GREAT CHAIN METAPHOR functions in our understanding of our relation to the cosmos. Let us now turn to a case where that same metaphor functions in our understanding of our relation to society.

> Knife can't whittle
> its own handle

Here again we have a description of a source domain with no indicator of the target domain. But since we know it is a proverb, we know that it must be about human affairs. The schematic knowledge about knives that is assumed here is: a knife consists of a blade and a handle; the handle of each knife is whittled; whittling involves using a knife. The proverb is particularly interesting because it reminds us of something we already know, namely, that a knife cannot be used to whittle its own handle, which entails that another knife is needed. And of course, since that knife could not whittle its own handle either, still another knife is needed, and so on.

The generic-level information in the schema is that *the form of one thing is brought into existence by the prolonged gradual repeated action of something of the same type.* The GREAT CHAIN METAPHOR links this to human affairs. People are "shaped" by society through their regular interactions with other people, from their immediate families to the society as a whole. The GREAT CHAIN METAPHOR maps the "shaping" of one knife by another onto the shaping of one person by another. Knives correspond to people. The shape of the handle corresponds to the character of the person. The prolonged gradual repeated action of the whittling knife corresponds to the prolonged gradual repeated action of other people in society who metaphorically "shape" what we are. The physical force with which the shaping is done corresponds to the force of social interaction. The moral is that there are essential parts of oneself that can only be shaped with the help of other people.

Society here is seen as a form of being in itself. Part of its essential nature is that it consists of the interactions of individuals with one another, and so the workings of society are by nature interactional. Society too can operate with force, metaphorically understood in terms of lower-order physical forces. On the Great Chain, society is a step above the level of individual people and a step below the level of the cosmos.

Extensions of the Great Chain and Their Social and Political Consequences

The cultural model of the Great Chain concerns not merely attributes and behavior but also dominance. In this cultural model, higher forms of being dominate lower forms of being by virtue of their higher natures. Humans dominate animals: "And God said . . . Let them have dominion over the fish of the sea, and over the fowl of the air, and over the cattle, and over all the earth, and over every creeping thing that creepeth upon the earth" (Genesis 1, 26). Similarly, we conventionally think it natural that people be subject to the ways of their society. And whether one uses a word like "cosmos" or not, most people assume that there are some natural ways that things work in the world and that everything, from lower forms of being to people to societies, conforms to them.

For example, when the Athenians are explaining to the Melians why it is natural that the Melian society should submit to the Athenian empire, they say, "Our opinion of the gods and our knowledge of men leads us to conclude that it is a general and necessary law of nature to rule whatever one can" (Thucydides, bk. 5, chap. 105). The Athenians are explaining that they are acting in accord with a natural law that applies to societies and that the Melians, being the weaker, should not talk about justice between societies but rather submit to the natural law that, between societies, might makes right. This same principle underlay the notion in the nineteenth century that America had a "manifest destiny" to expand its borders at the expense of weaker nations around it.

The basic form of the Great Chain that we have sketched so far is skeletal. It is what is unconsciously taken for granted in a wide variety of cultures. But the Great Chain, as it developed in the West, was much more elaborate. To the basic Great Chain there was added the Cultural Model of Macrocosm and Microcosm: each level of the chain was expanded to reflect the structure of the chain as a whole. At each level, there were higher and lower forms of being, with the higher forms dominating the lower.

For example, in the animal kingdom, lions, grizzly bears, and birds of prey are higher beings—the lions in terrestrial Africa and Europe, the grizzly bears in terrestrial North America, and the birds of prey in the air. They dominate lower forms like gazelles, deer, and snakes.

The human level was also given an internal hierarchy, with the king above the nobility, the nobility above the peasants, men above women, adults above children, and masters over slaves.

The cosmic level too could be given its internal hierarchy. For example, the Greek gods had a role in determining the nature of the cosmos, and they formed a loose hierarchy, with Zeus above the other Olympians, and the Olympians above lesser deities. But above Zeus and the Olympians were even stronger cosmic supernatural forces, such as the Fates. Zeus himself was obliged to obey the Fates in their determination that his son, Sarpedon, had to die.

In elaborations of Christian theology, the cosmos was determined by the divine order. At the top was God. Beneath him came Christ, and then the archangels, and then seven levels of angels, with the seraphim at the very top, the cherubim second, and so on. Below this cosmic level, in the religious extension of the Great Chain, the church constituted a social microcosm of the cosmic level: the pope was God's viceroy on earth, and beneath him came cardinals, then archbishops, then bishops, and so on.

The existence of these global and microcosmic hierarchies in the cultural model of the Great Chain, and in its conscious elaborations in the West, has had profound social and political consequences, because the cultural model indicates that the Great Chain is a description not merely of what hierarchies happen to *exist* in the world but, further, of what the hierarchies in the world *should be*. This implies that it is *wrong* to attempt to subvert this order of dominance. For example, it has been assumed that man should follow God, and woman should follow man, because the Great Chain indicates that this order of dominance is natural. As Eve says to Adam in *Paradise Lost*, book four:

> My Author and Disposer, what thou bidst
> Unargu'd I obey; so God ordains,
> God is thy Law, thou mine: to know no more
> Is woman's happiest knowledge and her praise.

Indeed, as we see here, the cultural model of the Great Chain includes the notion that dominance according to the Great Chain is at the essence of the cosmos and that to subvert that dominance in any microcosm is to challenge the correct order of the macrocosm. Consider, for example:

> The rats decide
> the cat ought to be belled.

By virtue of the cultural model of the Great Chain, we know that cats dominate rats. This implies that it is natural and correct for cats to dominate rats, and therefore that rats attempting to control the cat are subverting a microcosmic natural order, affronting the cosmic principles of right and wrong. The obvious interpretation of this proverb uses the GREAT CHAIN METAPHOR to give the reading that humans of lesser rank inappropriately and wrongfully attempt to control their natural masters.

A similar interpretation on the basis of the GREAT CHAIN METAPHOR can be given for:

> Cows run with the wind
> horses against it.

We know by virtue of the cultural model of the extended Great Chain that horses are higher and hence nobler than cows. Therefore, what this proverb says in this interpretation is that it is nobler, metaphorically, to counter social forces than to conform to them.

The influence of the extended Great Chain on our social and political beliefs and behavior is not merely a historical matter; it dominates much of contemporary social and political behavior. For example, the "third world" was originally called "third" to indicate that it was politically nonaligned, but now "third" is widely taken in industrialized societies as indicating a status inferior to the industrialized world and naturally to be dominated by it, just as it seemed natural to the Athenians that they should dominate the Melians. Nations that are not industrialized and are therefore less powerful than industrialized nations are considered "underdeveloped," as if the only criterion for "development" were industrialization and power over other nations.

In all contemporary societies, the more powerful classes of people are called the "upper" classes and are usually considered to be better than the "lower" classes. In India, the Great Chain is extended at the level of society into a caste system with the Brahmins at the top and the Untouchables at the bottom. This caste system is a microcosm reflecting the cosmic Great Chain, and it is understood metaphorically in terms of another microcosm reflecting the Great Chain, namely, the human body: the Brahmins are the head, the Untouchables are the feet, and the other castes fall between. Just as the head, according to the Great Chain, is and should be in control of the rest of the body, so, the metaphor goes, the Brahmins are and should be dominant over lower castes.

The extended version of the Great Chain obviously has ethical, social, political, and even religious consequences, as in the case of India's caste system, or in the notions that men should dominate women and that more powerful nations have a right and obligation to rule less powerful nations.

Many consequences of the extended Great Chain have been named, described, and denounced. Many political revolutions have been fought to rid a society of some part of the extended Great Chain. Even the partly extended Great Chain spanning the cosmos, society, human beings, animals, plants, and the physical world also and less obviously has ethical, social, and political consequences. The notions that the state has dominion over the individual and that human beings have a natural right to use animals and the earth as they see fit without regard for the integrity of nature have been challenged as unethical or evil.

The ecology movement, noting the dependence of all forms of living beings on the physical environment and our dependence on the food chain and on the existence of biological diversity, has proposed an inversion of the Great Chain, speaking of the "rights of the earth." Some members of the ecology movement have observed that there are now, and have existed in the past, cultures with a form of religion reflecting an inverted Great Chain. Some animistic religions, for example, see deities in aspects of the natural world, such as rivers, mountain ranges, and crop-bearing land. These aspects of the natural world are therefore divine, which puts them at the cosmic level, above us, requiring of us that they be revered, respected, and treated well. Such religions, it is sometimes claimed, might serve us better in the long run than our current ones.

But even the ecology movement is, in the main, influenced by the Great Chain as it stands. It is common for us to hear that we should save the whale because it is such a noble animal, or that it would be a great loss for the majestic Siberian tiger or the indomitable bald eagle to become extinct. These adjectives—"noble," "majestic," and so on— indicate that we are being asked to preserve these animals because they are higher and therefore better. Such arguments are persuasive because they depend upon the cultural model of the Great Chain. It is much harder to persuade people that it would be terrible to lose the lowly snail darter, because the snail darter's position in the Great Chain makes it culturally insignificant.

For whatever reason, perhaps because in our early cognitive development we inevitably form the model of the basic Great Chain as we interact with the world, it seems that the Great Chain is widespread and has strong natural appeal. This is frightening. It implies that those social, political, and ecological evils induced by the Great Chain will not disappear quickly or easily or of their own accord.

The Great Chain itself is a political issue. As a chain of dominance, it can become a chain of subjugation. It extends over centuries, linking the causes of anticolonial Americans and antiroyalist French to those still bound by it—from Blacks to women to Untouchables to aborigines to the environment, from whales and eagles to snails and species of lettuce, to the integrity of rivers.

Conclusion

To study metaphor is to be confronted with hidden aspects of one's own mind and one's own culture. To understand poetic metaphor, one must understand conventional metaphor. To do so is to discover that one has a worldview, that one's imagination is constrained, and that metaphor plays an enormous role in shaping one's everyday understanding of everyday events. That is an important part of the power of poetic metaphor: it calls upon our deepest modes of everyday understanding and forces us to use them in new ways.

It is vital that we understand our own worldviews and the processes that guide both our everyday understanding and our imagination. This book is in the service of that goal. It is in the service of helping the study of poetry function to promote ethical, social, and personal awareness.

We cannot have an appreciation of how metaphorical thought functions either in literature or in our lives without a rudimentary knowledge of what metaphor is and how it works. For this reason, we have taken the pains to spell out as many details as is feasible in a short book.

Recent discoveries about the nature of metaphor suggest that metaphor is anything but peripheral to the life of the mind. It is central to our understanding of our selves, our culture, and the world at large. Poetry, through metaphor, exercises our minds so that we can extend our normal powers of comprehension beyond the range of the metaphors we are brought up to see the world through.

The Western tradition, which has excluded metaphor from the domain of reason, has thereby relegated poetry and art to the periphery of intellectual life—something to give one a veneer of culture, but not something of central value in one's everyday endeavors. Part of our goal is to change that aspect of the Western tradition, and to do so through the empirical, scientific study of language and thought. This book is a contribution to that endeavor.

If there is a villain in the Western philosophical tradition, it is the Literal Meaning Theory. That theory has, for two millennia, defined meaningfulness, reason, and truth so as to exclude metaphor and other aspects of what Mark Johnson has called "imaginative rationality." In doing so, it claims that metaphor plays no role in the serious matters of life; it can at best serve as ornamentation or perhaps play a role in irrational persuasion. This has led to the mistaken notion that metaphor is something that belongs only to poets, and that the work of poets, while entertaining, is not serious, and that poetry is a strange, escapist sort of activity, alienated from our everyday lives.

We have now seen that, on the contrary, poetic metaphor, far from being ornamentation, deals with central and indispensable aspects of our conceptual systems. Through the masterful use of metaphoric processes on which our conceptual systems are based, poets address the most vital issues in our lives and help us illuminate those issues, through the extension, composition, and criticism of the basic metaphoric tools through which we comprehend much of reality.

Poets can appeal to the ordinary metaphors we live by in order to take us beyond them, to make us more insightful than we would be if we thought only in the standard ways. Because they lead us to new ways of conceiving of our world, poets are artists of the mind.

There is an ancient and unbroken debate over whether poetry is misleading fancy to be dismissed or truth to be studied. The terms of this debate are mistaken: poets are *both* imaginative and truthful.

In Shakespeare's *Midsummer Night's Dream*, Theseus takes a position reminiscent of a literal meaning theorist, arguing that poets are like lovers and madmen: they are fanciful and therefore misperceive the truth. Hippolyta correctly sees that Theseus's dichotomy is mistaken: poets see more than "fancy's images," something that "grows to great constancy." We think that the evidence is on the side of Hippolyta.

HIPPOLYTA: 'Tis strange, my Theseus, that these lovers speak of.
THESEUS: More strange than true; I never may believe
    These antique fables, nor these fairy toys.
    Lovers and madmen have such seething brains,
    Such shaping fantasies, that apprehend
    More than cool reason ever comprehends.
    The lunatic, the lover, and the poet
    Are of imagination all compact.
    One sees more devils than vast hell can hold;
    That is, the madman. The lover, all as frantic,
    Sees Helen's beauty in a brow of Egypt.
    The poet's eye, in a fine frenzy rolling,
    Doth glance from heaven to earth, from earth to heaven;
    And as imagination bodies forth
    The forms of things unknown, the poet's pen
    Turns them to shapes and gives to airy nothing
    A local habitation and a name.
    Such tricks hath strong imagination,
    That, if it would but apprehend some joy,
    It comprehends some bringer of that joy;
    Or in the night, imagining some fear,
    How easy is a bush suppos'd a bear!
HIPPOLYTA: But all the story of the night told over,
    And all their minds transfigur'd so together,
    More witnesseth than fancy's images,
    And grows to something of great constancy;
    But, howsoever, strange and admirable.

More on Traditional Views

For those who wish to read works in lively contemporary traditions by authors who hold the traditional views of metaphor discussed in chapter two, here are some suggestions as to where to start.

Jerrold Sadock's essay "Figurative Speech and Linguistics" takes the Literal Meaning Theory for granted. When Sadock argues that "All nonliteral speech, then, including metaphor, falls outside the domain of synchronic linguistics . . ." (p. 46), he is assuming a version of the Literal Meaning Theory in which purely literal thought and expression of philosophical ideas is possible and in which metaphor is a distortion of the literal. David Rumelhart's "Some Problems with the Notion of Literal Meanings" takes a view more congenial to the view expressed in this book. Both essays appear in *Metaphor and Thought*, ed. Andrew Ortony (Cambridge: Cambridge University Press, 1979).

The Pragmatics Position, which presupposes the Literal Meaning Theory, was first proposed by philosopher Paul Grice in his 1967 Harvard lectures on conversational implicature and appeared in print in Grice's paper "Logic and Conversation" in *Speech Acts*, ed. Peter Cole and Jerry L. Morgan, Syntax and Semantics Series, vol. 3 (New York: Academic Press, 1975). Grice's work was an attempt to preserve the view that natural language semantics could be handled by formal logic, provided that a theory of conversational principles was added. Since metaphor is beyond the capacities of formal logic, metaphor had to be handled, on Grice's view, by conversational principles operating on literal meanings. John Searle expanded on Grice's views in his 1979 paper "Metaphor" in *Metaphor and Thought*. And

Dan Sperber and Deirdre Wilson provide another version in their book, *Relevance* (Oxford: Basil Blackwell, 1986).

The No Concepts Position is primarily associated with philosophers Donald Davidson and Richard Rorty. In his classic essay, "What Metaphors Mean," Davidson adopts a version of the literal meaning theory in which "metaphors mean what the words, in their most literal interpretation mean, and nothing more." But Davidson's theory of meaning is a No Concepts theory, in which meaning is based on truth, but not conceptual understanding. For a discussion, see Davidson's classic "On the very idea of a conceptual scheme," in *Proceedings and Addresses of the American Philosophical Association,* 67 (1973–4), p 5—20. Rorty, who has rejected the view of concepts as mirroring aspects of reality, finds Davidson's views on meaning and metaphor congenial. He specifically adopts Davidson's views on metaphor in his three "Contingency" essays in the *London Review of Books*, April 17, May 8, and July 24, 1986. Rorty also explicitly adopts the Dead Metaphor Position in those essays.

The Interactionist Theory is attributed to I. A. Richards in "The Philosophy of Rhetoric" and Max Black in "Metaphor." Both are reprinted in *Philosophical Perspectives on Metaphor,* ed. Mark Johnson (Minneapolis: University of Minnesota Press, 1981). The It's All Metaphor Position is, of course, due to Friedrich Nietzsche, "On Truth and Falsity in their Ultramoral Sense" (1873), in *The Complete Works of Friedrich Nietzsche*, ed. Oscar Levy, trans. Maximilian A. Magge (New York: Gordon Press, 1974). Here is Nietzsche's most notable passage on metaphor:

> What therefore is truth? A mobile army of metaphors, metonymies, anthropomorphisms: in short a sum of human relations which become poetically and rhetorically intensified, metamorphosed, adorned, and after long usage seem to a nation fixed, canonic and binding; truths are illusions of which one has forgotten that they *are* illusions; worn-out metaphors which have become powerless to affect the senses . . . (p. 80).

Bibliography

Poetic Works Cited

Amichai, Yehuda. *Selected Poetry of Yehuda Amichai*. Edited and translated by Chana Bloch and Stephen Mitchell. New York: Harper and Row, 1986.

Auster, Paul, ed. *The Random House Book of Twentieth-Century French Poetry*. New York: Random House, 1984.

Merwin, W. S. *Asian Figures*. New York: Atheneum, 1973.

Merwin, W. S., and J. Moussaieff Masson, trans. *Sanskrit Love Poetry*. New York: Columbia University Press, 1977. Reprinted as *The Peacock's Egg*. San Francisco: North Point Press, 1981.

Rothenberg, Jerome, ed. *Technicians of the Sacred*. Berkeley and Los Angeles: University of California Press, 1985.

Further Works on Metaphor

Brugman, Claudia. "Metaphor in the Elaboration of Grammatical Categories in Mixtec." Unpublished manuscript.

Johnson, Mark. *Philosophical Perspectives on Metaphor*. Minneapolis: University of Minnesota Press, 1981.

———. *The Body in the Mind. The Bodily Basis of Meaning, Reason and Imagination*. Chicago: University of Chicago Press, 1987.

Lakoff, George. *Women, Fire, and Dangerous Things: What Categories Reveal about the Mind*. Chicago: University of Chicago Press, 1987.

Lakoff, George and Mark Johnson. *Metaphors We Live By*. Chicago: University of Chicago Press, 1980.

Holland, Dorothy, and Naomi Quinn, eds. *Cultural Models in Language and Thought*. Cambridge: Cambridge University Press, 1987.

Nagy, William. "Figurative Patterns and Redundancy in the Lexicon." Ph.D. diss., University of California at San Diego, 1974.

Ortony, Andrew, ed. *Metaphor and Thought*. Cambridge: Cambridge University Press, 1979.

Reddy, Michael. "The Conduit Metaphor" in *Metaphor and Thought*. Edited by Andrew Ortony. Cambridge: Cambridge University Press, 1979).

Ricoeur, Paul. *The Rule of Metaphor*. Translated by Robert Czerny. Toronto: University of Toronto Press, 1977.

Sacks, Sheldon, ed. *On Metaphor*. Chicago: University of Chicago Press, 1977.

Sweetser, Eve. *From Etymology to Pragmatics: The Mind–as–Body Metaphor in Semantic Structure and Semantic Change*. Cambridge: Cambridge University Press, in press.

Thompson, Ann and John O. Thompson. *Shakespeare: Meaning and Metaphor*. Brighton: The Harvester Press, 1987.

Turner, Mark. *Death is the Mother of Beauty: Mind, Metaphor, Criticism*. Chicago: University of Chicago Press, 1987.

Index of Metaphors

Index of Topics